'Assassinations... our poisoned chalice'

SHAKESPEARE

ON ASSASSINATIONS

KENNETH BAKER

UNICORN

*I dedicate this book to P.D. Whiting,
my history tutor at St Paul's,
who inspired me to love history.*

CONTENTS

INTRODUCTION

In *Macbeth* Shakespeare for the first time in a major literary work uses the word 'assassination', to assess its effect as Macbeth considers whether he should murder Duncan, the King of Scotland, who is a guest staying at his castle. If the assassination could work like a net sweeping up everything without any consequences then he had better get on with it as quickly as possible. But there may be consequences, for if one resorts to violence others will respond violently.

> If it were done when 'tis done, then 'twere well
> It were done quickly. If the assassination
> Could trammel up the consequence, and catch
> With his surcease success; that but this blow
> Might be the be-all and end-all here,
> But here, upon this bank and shoal of time,
> We'd jump the life to come. But in these cases
> We still have judgment here, that we but teach
> Bloody instructions, which, being taught, return
> To plague th'inventor: this even-handed justice
> Commends the ingredients of our poisoned chalice
> To our own lips.

It takes the genius of Shakespeare to foresee the dilemma that faces all assassins. They hope that by killing their target they will remove someone who is a threat, a rival, an over-powerful figure, an evil person, and the world will recognise that what they have done was right and just. That is rarely the reaction to an assassination, for in most cases the consequence is the complete opposite to what the assassin had hoped, and so it was for Macbeth. After his wife had persuaded him to kill the King, fulfilling the witches' prophecy, Duncan's son with the support of other Scottish nobles marched on Macbeth's castle. 'Bloody instructions, which, being taught, return to plague th'inventor': Duncan's assassination was a poisoned chalice.

Shakespeare placed Julius Caesar's assassination on the Ides of March in 44 BC at the centre of his play, dramatising its preparation, its execution and its consequences. Although Caesar had refused a kingship offered three times by Mark Antony, he had all the trappings of regal power – a golden seat in the Senate and his image on the coinage – and he gave scant regard to the ancient liberties and practices of the Roman Republic. A group of senators and friends led by Brutus

Royal Shakespeare Company 2017

and Cassius decided to kill him, and he was stabbed twenty-three times. Brutus then called out 'Liberty! Freedom! Tyranny is dead!' and Cassius concluded:

> So often shall the knot of us be call'd
> The men that gave their country liberty.

But the reading of Caesar's will at the public funeral turned the plebs against the assassins and launched a catastrophic civil war. Brutus and Cassius fled to Greece and built up an army, and Octavian, adopted by Caesar as his son and heir, defeated them at the Battle of Philippi in 42 BC. Cassius was the first to commit suicide, and a few days later Brutus fell upon his sword. For them Caesar's assassination was definitely a poisoned chalice.

For the next eleven years Octavian and Mark Antony vied for power, and in 31 BC Octavian destroyed the combined fleets of Antony and Cleopatra at the Battle of Actium. This battle marked the end of the Roman Republic and the beginning of Imperial Rome. Thirteen years after the assassination of Julius Caesar, the purpose of which was to prevent power falling into the hands of one man, that is exactly what happened. Octavian adopted the title of 'Princeps Civitatis' (First Citizen), and he became the first emperor, awarding himself the title 'Augustus', with powers much wider than those enjoyed by Julius Caesar.

All assassins believe that by killing their target they will change the world, or at least their part of it. Benjamin Disraeli did not agree. He told the House of Commons in 1865: 'Assassination has never changed the history of the world.' Any assassination of a leading political figure is such an unexpected and dramatic event that it hits the headlines, and the sheer violence of the death evokes sympathy for the victim and revulsion towards the assassins. Within days rumours begin to fly around as to whether there was a wider conspiracy involving many others and how one person acting alone could possibly have done it. All this makes an assassination more important than in fact it is, and it is not surprising that such a tragic drama raises the expectation that it will be a turning point. But in many cases another leader either legitimately or illegitimately emerges and makes reassuring promises about stability and continuity.

As I have personally known eight colleagues and friends who were assassinated and whose deaths did not change history, I wanted to explore whether the assassination of other public figures had resulted in a poisoned chalice for the assassin and whether any had really changed the history of the world. My friends were Ian Gow MP, assassinated by the IRA, the Irish Republican Army; Airey Neave MP, by the INLA, the Irish National Liberation Army, the militant arm of the Irish Republican Socialist Party, a splinter group from Sinn Fein; Ross McWhirter by the IRA; Tony Berry MP and Roberta Wakeham by the IRA, who planted a bomb in the hotel in Brighton, the town hosting the Conservative Party Conference, with the intention of killing Margaret Thatcher; Lalith Athulatmudali, the leader of the Sri Lankan Democratic United National Front, killed probably by the Tamil Tigers, though some alleged it was the killer squad of the Prime Minister Premadasa who was himself assassinated a week later; Laksham Kadirgamar, the Foreign Secretary of Sri Lanka, who, although a Tamil, was shot by a Tamil Tiger sniper; and Richard Sharples, a former Member of Parliament and Minister, sailing companion of Ted Heath and Governor of Bermuda, where he was killed by a black nationalist.

Two of these eight were close personal friends – Ian Gow and Tony Berry. Ian and his family were neighbours of ours in Sussex and we saw a great deal of each other. Ian Gow, almost prophetically, condemned another terrorist outrage just a week before his own murder: 'Once again wives have been turned into widows and children into orphans. And for what purpose?' What purpose indeed. The IRA claimed credit for his 'execution' but it did nothing to further their cause.

I knew Tony Berry through playing bridge with him during those long nights when the House of Commons sat late, often into the next day. I was particularly saddened by his death. I may have been the last politician he talked to, as I had to leave the Conservative Party conference for an early morning debate in London with Ken Livingstone on the abolition of the Greater London Council. So Mary and I left the Imperial Hotel around 1.30am, and as we were going down the hotel steps we met Tony, who had been taking his small dog for a walk along the promenade. We chatted about the conference and how the Government was going through a very bad patch – rising unemployment, the Miners' Strike, Tory-shire MPs up in arms about high council rates, and Livingstone and Derek Hatton running rings around us in local government. As Deputy Chief Whip he was relieved: 'Thank Heavens we've had a good conference and Margaret will top it off today' – a speech he was not to hear, as he was killed two hours later. He had never been involved in Northern Ireland issues, but then the IRA never cared about how many innocent people they murdered.

I also knew two of my fellow MPs who had narrowly escaped assassination attempts. Christopher Tugendhat had become a close colleague in the House of Commons where he represented the Cities of London and Westminster South while I was the MP for Marylebone and Westminster North. He was appointed by the Labour Prime Minister, James Callaghan, to be a European Commissioner. In 1980 he narrowly escaped being assassinated while leaving his house with his wife in Brussels when an IRA terrorist fired three bullets that hit the door jamb at his side and above him. He was inches away from death. Another MP, Hugh Fraser, escaped assassination when a bomb planted under his car was accidentally set off by a passer-by just as Hugh was leaving his house to go to his car accompanied by Caroline Kennedy, the daughter of President Kennedy. Both would have been killed.

I have also met three other people who were assassinated, but they were not personal friends. They were Lord Mountbatten, Indira Gandhi, and her son, Rajiv Gandhi. When Mrs Gandhi came to London she invariably had dinner with Margaret Thatcher, and although they were politically miles apart there was a great deal of mutual respect, for they had both graduated from Somerville College in Oxford and had become the female leaders of their countries. It was at these dinners that I met Mrs Gandhi and her son.

All of these victims were public servants serving their country and in some cases their constituents. They were not evil or cruel people who would be better out of this world. They were victims of terrorist groups committed to achieving their ends through violence, with the belief that their cause would be enhanced by assassinating some of their preeminent opponents. Quite the reverse, for these bloody deaths evoked revulsion, disgust, and a renewed determination that such murders should achieve nothing. The IRA, INLA and the Tamil Tigers were terrorist organisations which all failed to achieve their objectives.

So I decided to look at other assassinations of significant figures across the world to see whether they carried with them the seeds of their own defeat and whether any had affected the course of history. I kept a record of assassinations as they occurred – for they continue to happen – and I have looked at well over one hundred historic ones. I decided not to include the Roman emperors: of the seventy-one emperors thirty-one had been assassinated, as that had become the route to replace one dictator by another (see Appendix 2). The assassins were usually from the Praetorian Guard, the elite soldiers charged with the task of protecting the emperor. It was also for them a source of making money, and in some years the office of emperor was put up for auction and went to the highest bidder. Gibbon described brilliantly the impermanence of imperial rule and how it contributed to the Decline and Fall of Rome. The year AD 238 was known as 'The Year of the Six Emperors'. One of these was Gordian II, who lasted only a month before being killed in battle by Maximinus Thrax. Gordian inspired one of Gibbon's great ironic dismissals: 'Twenty-two acknowledged concubines and a library of sixty-two thousand volumes attested the variety of his inclinations, and from the productions he left behind him it appears that the former as well as the latter were designed for use rather than ostentation.'

Nor have I attempted to chart all the assassinations in the history of the Ottoman Empire, where the best way of retaining power was to kill all other claimants. This practice was supported by a verse in the Koran: 'The execution of a prince is preferable to the loss of a province.' Fratricide was stopped in the seventeenth century after Mehmed III had secured his accession by having nineteen of his brothers and half-brothers strangled.

Individual Assassins

Before the middle of the twentieth century most assassinations were carried out by an individual acting alone who planned to kill a specific person, in a specific place, at a specific time. Assassins tend to be lonely individuals, and their isolation and their resentment rankle and fester over the years, turning into an implacable hatred of the victim that becomes the burning passion of their lives. There is no such thing as a cool and calculating assassin. Since 1945 assassinations by individuals have become rarer, and most assassinations have been carried out by agents operating for a state.

The period 1882–1914 has been called the Golden Age of Assassinations. It was characterised by many assassinations carried out by individuals: President Carnot of France in 1894, Prime Minister Cánovas of Spain in 1897, the Empress Elizabeth of Austria in 1898, King Umberto of Italy in 1900, President McKinley of America in 1901, King Carlos of Portugal and his heir in 1908, Prime Minister Stolypin of Russia in 1911, King George I of Greece in 1913, and Archduke Franz Ferdinand in Sarajevo in 1914.

Several of these assassins were anarchists. Anarchism had become a major terrorist creed, just as militant Islam has become today. It was founded on the writing of the nineteenth-century French philosopher and politician Pierre-Joseph Proudhon, who believed that if all authority and property ownership were abolished a society would emerge based on voluntary activity leading to social harmony. Today anarchism is an irrelevant political force, which unfortunately militant Islam is not.

Assassins are quite frequently described as being cowardly, as some sneak close to their victims to catch them off guard. Nothing could be further from the truth: they have to be courageous, determined and resourceful, knowing full well that they themselves may be killed immediately or executed later. Take Charlotte Corday, the middle-class assassin from Normandy: passionate, determined, fearless, focused upon her target, quite prepared to sacrifice her own life, she was utterly convinced that what she was going to do would make the world a better place. It became the mission of her life. She was appalled that

Jean Joseph Weerts, *L'Assassinat de Marat*

some of her friends had been guillotined by the extreme Jacobins in Paris, whom she described as 'nothing but common executioners'. She went alone to Paris, bought a butcher's knife for two francs, and on 13 July 1793 boldly knocked on the door of Jean Marat, one of the celebrated Jacobins who compiled daily death-lists published in his newspaper to keep the mob on his side. She was about to be turned away when Marat heard her voice and told his servants to let her in.

Marat was sitting in a large metal bathtub filled with warm water to relieve the irritation of his skin disease (this might have been caught when he went into hiding in the sewers of Paris, but later doctors have claimed that it was an extreme case of herpes). Corday won his attention by naming some of the Girondins in Normandy. He added them to his death-list, saying, 'I shall send them all to the guillotine in a few days.' She then drew out her butcher's knife and plunged it into his chest. She was arrested, tried immediately, and guillotined four days later. When asked if she had anything to say she replied, 'Nothing except that I have succeeded.' Before she was guillotined she was painted by Jean-Jacques Hauer, and she sent a letter to a friend in Caen 'I long to be with Brutus in the Elysian fields.' Very courageous, but ineffective: by killing Marat she hoped to end the guillotining of so many, but within weeks Robespierre won control of the Revolutionary Committee and launched the Great Terror, in which 300,000 were arrested and 17,000 guillotined.

Other solitary assassins were mentally deranged, in some cases certifiable lunatics. One head of government killed by a lunatic was the Prime Minister of South Africa, Hendrik Verwoerd, in 1966, stabbed by a parliamentary messenger fed up with his low pay. Four American presidents were shot at by lunatics – Andrew Jackson, Theodore Roosevelt, Gerald Ford and Ronald Reagan. George III was attacked by three lunatics: a lady with a blunt knife attacked him as he was entering St James's Palace, another aimed a pistol shot when he was at his box in the Drury Lane Theatre, and the third when he was reviewing some troops. Queen Victoria was attacked seven times, usually while she was travelling in an open coach with virtually no guards. Most of her would-be assassins were mentally disturbed.

Other individual assassins had a personal grudge. The only British Prime Minister to be assassinated was Spencer Perceval, shot when entering the House of Commons in 1812 by John Bellingham, a disgruntled businessman, who held the Prime Minister responsible for his failure in a venture in Russia. John Felton, who shot Charles I's leading minister, the Duke of Buckingham, in 1628, was an officer who was heavily in debt and who had been passed over for promotion. President Garfield was shot in 1881 by a man who had not been appointed ambassador to Austria, a post for which he was totally unsuited. Such assassinations are unpredictable and impossible to guard against.

The period since the end of the Second World War has seen a relatively small number of individual assassins. The notable exceptions are Lee Harvey Oswald who shot President Kennedy and Sirhan Sirhan who killed his brother Robert Kennedy; James Earl Ray, who had no accomplice or fellow conspirator when he shot Martin Luther King; and Thomas Mair, a mentally disturbed racist who shot Jo Cox, the English MP. All these assassins were not members of a wider movement: they were solitary killers who had persuaded themselves that they had a duty to rid the world of their victim and they showed no remorse, being utterly confident that what they had done was the right thing.

1945–2019: the era of state targeted killings

The period since the Second World War has been dominated by states using assassinations to remove dissidents and investigative journalists representing a threat to their power. Killings undertaken by a state are usually carried out by the security services or armed forces. In the twenty-first century targeted killings have been undertaken by the following countries: Russia, Israel, America, Syria, Saudi Arabia, India, Malta, Romania, Slovakia, Bulgaria, the Ukraine, and even Great Britain. Five of these countries are in the European Union.

Two countries use assassination as a matter of policy. Russia does it to keep Putin and his entourage of supporters in power. Israel does it to protect its national security, since several Arab countries would gladly assist in its obliteration. Since its foundation in 1948 Israel has planned and implemented more assassinations that any other country, for it has to remain on a constant war footing to protect its citizens from rocket attacks from Gaza or suicide bombers crossing the border. Israel's targets have been the leaders of Hamas and the designers and manufacturers of bombs, and the long arm of Mossad has reached out to kill in countries including Tunisia and Malaysia.

Leaders of repressive regimes often use assassination to remove rivals. Hitler used Himmler and Goering to murder his old colleague Ernst Röhm. Putin in 2017, facing an election, ensured that his most effective opponent, Boris Nemtsov, a former Deputy Prime Minister, was first banned from standing by a trumped-up corruption charge and then shot as he walked with his fiancée over a bridge near the Kremlin.

Investigative journalists from Bulgaria, Russia, Malta, India, Slovakia, the Ukraine and Saudi Arabia have been assassinated to protect the ruling regime from the exposure of corrupt senior politicians, the rigging of elections, and the promotion of cronies and family members. In 2019 a journalist in Ghana was shot dead after he exposed football corruption, and two Afghan journalists were assassinated in their radio studios. The news of these assassinations does leak out across the world, as the killing of one reporter does not silence their colleagues. In the case of the journalist Ján Kuciak, who together with his fiancée was murdered in Slovakia in 2018 owing to his investigations of Mafia corruption of government ministers, his editor responded by saying: 'Our message is that if you kill a journalist more information will come out. They can't kill all of us.' Within three weeks more information did come out, and the Prime Minister of Slovakia was forced to resign, though he is still thought to be the main manipulator of politics in that country. In Russia the free press has disappeared, and between 1993 and 2009 365 journalists and other people associated with the freedom of expression in the media were murdered. The leading investigative journalist who was exposing corruption in Chechnya, Anna Politkovskya, was shot in the lift of her apartment block.

So far the only leading politician who has been assassinated this century in Europe is Alexander Zakharchenko, leader of the breakaway territory in the Ukraine, who was killed by a bomb in 2018 in a restaurant in Donetsk, almost certainly on Russian orders.

Targeted killings by political terrorists

Terrorist groups such as the IRA, INLA, the Red Brigade and the Tamil Tigers have all engaged in targeted killings. They were all seeking publicity for their causes and believed that the more they killed the better, but such excessive violence and the killing of innocent people including children engendered only anger, hostility and rejection. Some of these assassinations, particularly those motivated by religious hatred, were directed at individuals, but the target was extended to include large numbers of civilians, so assassins mutated into terrorists.

From 1969 the IRA decided to promote its cause for a united Ireland by engaging in violent attacks, both in Northern Ireland and in Britain. Bombs were planted in public places: many innocent bystanders were killed in pubs in Guildford and Birmingham, and cavalry soldiers with their horses were killed in Hyde Park in London. The IRA soon realised that inflaming hostility among the ordinary public damaged their cause, and they moved to target individual British politicians and leading figures. Those assassinations were often carried out by a single person, like Patrick McGee, who planted the bomb in the Brighton hotel bedroom above that to be occupied by Margaret Thatcher while she was at the Conservative Party Conference; the unknown assassin who placed a bomb under the car outside Ian Gow's house in Sussex; another who placed a bomb under Airey Neave's car that blew up in the House of Commons car park; and Thomas McMahon, who decided to kill Lord Mountbatten and family members by hiding a bomb in the boat on which they were enjoying a family outing. Although these assassins acted alone, they had the backing of the IRA, which financed and supplied them with weapons. The IRA leaders knew exactly what was happening. Sometimes the IRA formed a small group, like the four who set off bombs in the West End of London in 1975 and then went on to shoot down Ross McWhirter when he opened his front door. That group were run to earth in the Balcombe Street siege.

In Italy in March 1978 the Red Brigade terrorist organisation kidnapped the Prime Minister, Aldo Moro, to prevent him forging an alliance between the great political parties – the Christian Democrats and the Socialist and Communist Parties. For over twenty years the Red Brigade had used violence, terrorist tactics and assassination to further their revolutionary aims, and that period was given the title of 'the Years of Lead'. Moro was kept captive for fifty-five days; the police never discovered where he was being held. When the Government would not negotiate or meet any of the Red Brigade's demands, they lost their patience and on 9 May they shot him and bundled his body into the boot of a car which was then parked midway between the headquarters of the Communists and the Christian Democrats. It was such an appalling murder that the full force of the Italian state, police and security services was directed to bringing thirty-two Red Brigade terrorists to trial. In 1983 the Red Brigade announced: 'The revolutionary

The death of a Prime Minister

struggle which started in the 1970s has finished – comrades must seek new means of revolution.' This assassination was certainly a poisoned chalice.

Targeted killings by religious terrorists

Religious terrorist groups such as ISIS, al-Qaeda, Fatah, Hamas, Hezbollah, the Muslim Brotherhood, Boko Haram in Nigeria and Jaish-e-Mohammed in Pakistan have all engaged in targeted killings, and they are more dangerous than political assassins since they are willing to embark on martyrdom missions. In the last fifteen years religious terrorists in the European capitals of Berlin, London, Madrid and Paris have killed 458 people and wounded 4,431.

These groups revel in the publicity for an attack, but they do not gain any support, in fact the opposite, as was the case with the attacks in London on 7 July 2005; the Manchester Arena bombing in 2017; and the murderous vehicles driven over Westminster Bridge and London Bridge in 2017. Many more attempts have been averted by the painstaking vigilance of MI5, whose task is to prevent or disrupt such murderous plots, and who at the time of the Manchester bombing was managing over 500 investigations involving some 3,000 people. That has probably risen, as some Jihadi fighters have returned to the UK from Syria and Iraq. Terrorists must not be allowed to win. Slowly but surely counter-terrorism will expose and defeat their plans.

People across the world are appalled by a minority of bigots preaching the most radical interpretation of their religion, slaughtering innocent victims, and distorting their religion to preach hatred rather than harmony and violence rather than virtue. These terrorist attacks make the headlines, but do not garner converts. The suicide bomber and other terrorist assassins will not bomb themselves into popularity.

This has been dramatically shown in the Middle East. On 5 July 2014 Abu Bakr al-Baghdadi, the leader of ISIS, in the Great Al-Nuri Mosque in the Iraq city of Mosul declared a new caliphate and announced that his footsoldiers had already captured land in Iraq and Syria to form an Islamic state. Assisted by 40,000 foreign fighters from over 110 countries, by the end of the year ISIS controlled a third of Iraq and a third of Syria. Many of the ISIS fighters worked in small groups, rapidly moving from one massacre to another, but some operated as individual assassins who devised new ways of killing – decapitation with a knife, drowning, burial alive, stoning, mutilation, being thrown off a roof or being crushed by a tank, and even crucified. Such savagery aroused the hostility of the world.

When ISIS publicly beheaded the US journalist James Foley in 2014; when they attacked the offices of the satirical magazine Charlie Hebdo in Paris in 2015; when a single soldier of the caliphate shot thirty British tourists in Tunisia; and when the British terrorist Jihadi John, identified as Mohammed Emwazi, videotaped the beheading of British citizens, the leaders of three countries – President Obama, President Hollande and Prime Minister Cameron – decided that ISIS must be crushed. By July 2019 an American-led coalition, which also included the Muslim President Erdogan of Turkey, and the Kurds, destroyed the caliphate: 50,000 ISIS soldiers were killed, making this the most successful counter-terrorist campaign the world has ever seen.

The evil deeds of such terrorist assassins promote repugnance, revulsion and a determination that they shall not succeed. As Margaret Thatcher said, 'They must never, never, never be allowed to triumph. They must not prevail.'

Good luck and bad luck

While targeted assassinations are more purposeful, planned events, individual assassinations seem rather more ad hoc, but I did find that both were subject to pure chance – good luck or bad luck. It can be the good luck of the assassin and the bad luck of the victim, or the reverse. Luck saved several people from being assassinated.

There is always a degree of uncertainty, since the intended victims may change their plans, choose a different route, or increase or remove their protection. As Cassius plans to kill Caesar he tells his fellow conspirators:

> . . . But it is doubtful yet,
> Whether Caesar will come forth today or not;
> For he is superstitious grown of late.

The Prime Minister Robert Peel was lucky that the assassin who wanted to kill him shot his Private Secretary Edward Drummond by mistake. Gavrilo Princip, the young Bosnian nationalist, had been planning for two years to assassinate the Archduke Franz Ferdinand, the heir to the Austro-Hungarian Empire. He could not believe his luck when the car of the Archduke took a wrong turning in Sarajevo: the driver was ordered to stop, and Princip found himself just 6 feet away. He did not aim specifically at the Archduke or his wife. He fired into the side of the car; his bullet went through the metal, wood and upholstery and ended up in the abdomen of the Duchess, killing her instantly. Princip had hardly ever fired a pistol; as it recoiled it was pointing up; in his trial he said he did not aim, looked away and just pulled the trigger. His second bullet passed through the neck of the Archduke, severing both the jugular vein and the carotid artery. If it had had a trajectory just one inch away the Archduke would not have been killed, and the First World War would not have started a month later.

President Mubarak of Egypt was very lucky not to be killed in the hail of bullets that killed President Sadat when they were both reviewing a military parade. There were thirty-one assassination attempts on Charles de Gaulle: in 1966 the would-be assassins had parked a car loaded with a tonne of dynamite on the boulevard Montparnasse where de Gaulle's car would pass on the following day; having primed the car they went off to commit a burglary to help fund their escape, and just by chance they were arrested by the police and the car with the bomb was discovered.

Marshal Tito was very lucky that the plan to assassinate him prepared by a cleverly disguised Russian agent was sent for Stalin's approval on 1 March 1953: in the early hours of the next day Stalin had a stroke and was to die four days later. Tito's life was saved by Stalin's death.

After his triumph in the presidential primary in Los Angeles on 5 June 1968 Robert Kennedy decided to leave the Ambassador Hotel not by the front entrance but by a service pantry leading to the back door, where, quite by chance, his assassin Sirhan Sirhan was waiting with a revolver, and he was shot.

The 'luckiest' escape was when Adolf Hitler on 8 November 1939 decided to leave a meeting in the Munich beer cellar where he had been speaking to old faithful Nazis. The assassin had planted a bomb in the pillar behind which he was to speak, assuming that he would leave at 10 o'clock, which he had always done at this annual meeting, and it was to detonate at 9:20pm – but Hitler decided to leave early, at 9:07pm, as the Second World War had already started. His life was saved by 13 minutes. If he had been killed that night the history of the world would have been very different.

The new weapons for assassinations

The traditional weapons of an assassin have been firearms, bombs, and more rarely knives and poison. An American report in 2007 looked at over three hundred assassinations of prominent people and found that although firearms were by far the most popular weapons they often failed. Bombs and grenades were condemned in a CIA pamphlet as being 'sloppy, unreliable and bad propaganda'. Two Czech nationalists planned to kill Heydrich, the leading Nazi, with a sten gun as his car drove around a hairpin bend, but it jammed; instead they had to throw a grenade at the car. Several of the assassins who shot at Queen Victoria were found to have loaded gunpowder rather than bullets in their pistols. Machine guns did not kill Trotsky: he was killed with a more unconventional and untried weapon, an ice axe. Stabbing was much more uncertain: Margaret Nicholson attacked George III with a blunt knife that did not even penetrate his coat. More recently, in 2018, the Brazilian presidential candidate Jair Bolsonaro was stabbed in his liver and lungs, but survived to win the election.

In the last twenty years two new weapons of assassination have been developed: the suicide bomb and the drone. These have already increased the scale of assassinations, one carried out by being very close to the victim and the other by remote control. The suicide vest was invented in 1996 by Ayyash, 'the Engineer', a bomb designer working for Hamas. He was so significant that the Prime Minister of Israel, Shimon Peres, approved his assassination, and his memory is venerated by Palestinians.

Only a suicide bomber can be assured that his victim will be killed. That is what happened to Rajiv Gandhi, who was killed by a woman concealing a bomb under her sari which she detonated when she stooped down to kiss his feet. The four terrorists from Yorkshire who on 7 July 2005 killed over 50 Londoners all wore suicide vests and made pre-recordings of what they were going to do. Suicide bombings still occur in Afghanistan and Iraq. In April 2018 for the first time a suicide bomber used a motorcycle to penetrate quickly into the most densely crowded area of a city. In the militant jihad/ISIS attacks in Sri Lanka in April 2019, which resulted in over 450 deaths and 500 injuries, the terrorists all wore suicide vests. Boko Haram came to regard football as 'un-Islamic' and the ultimate demonstration of corrupting Western influence. In January 2019 three suicide bombers killed 30 villagers and wounded many more while they were watching a football match on a screen outside the hall in Konduga, near the

A suicide bomber walking calmly to St. Sebastian's Church in Sri Lanka only moments before the deadly explosion at the Easter Sunday Service on 21 April 2019 when 259 Christians were killed.

state capital, Maiduguri. The biggest challenge to all societies is that terrorists regard it as a glorious way to die: some have called it 'the quickest way to Allah'.

Drones have been used extensively by governments to assassinate specific individuals in the Middle East, Afghanistan and Pakistan, raising significant ethical issues. On 5 August 2009 the CIA had tracked down Baitullah Mehsud (see pp. 203-204), a leading militant in Pakistan who organised attacks by his own army of fighters; one of his targets was said to have been Benazir Bhutto. He was killed by a drone, fully supported by the US Government and confirmed by President Obama with the words 'We took out Mehsud.'

Both America and Britain justify the killing of named individuals on the grounds of self-defence, since they could be planning attacks on American and British cities, even though they are not living in those countries. In 2010 a US

State Department lawyer, Harold Koh, justified attacks on those grounds. In 2015–16 the Joint Committee of Human Rights, in both the House of Lords and the House of Commons, tried to 'clarify the decision-making process that precedes any use of lethal force in circumstances such as those on 21 August 2015 in Syria'. This refers to a decision by Philip Hammond, the British Defence Secretary, to approve the killing of Reyaad Khan in Syria. David Cameron in the House of Commons on 7 September 2015 revealed the line of command and confirmed that the Attorney General had decided that this drone strike was legal:

> Our intelligence agencies identified the direct threat to the UK from this individual and informed me and other senior Ministers of that threat. At a meeting of the most senior members of the National Security Council, we agreed that should the right opportunity arise, military action should be taken. The Attorney General attended the meeting and confirmed that there was a legal basis for action. On that basis, the Defence Secretary authorised the operation. The strike was conducted according to specific military rules of engagement, which always comply with international law and the principles of proportionality and military necessity. The military assessed the target location and chose the optimum time to minimise the risk of civilian casualties.

From this it is clear that governments which have drones can use them as a political weapon to kill significant people who threaten their country's safety. These distant assassinations, when the person who presses the button can kill someone they have never seen, do raise moral questions. In times of war drones are simply another form of weapon, but in times of conflict short of war their use has been justified on the ground of self-defence, which can be quite a subjective decision. Perhaps David Cameron drew some comfort from Edmund Burke's comments in *Reflections on the Revolution in France* (1790): 'laws are commanded to hold their tongues amongst arms; and tribunals fall to the ground with the peace they are no longer able to uphold.'

The KGB in Russia developed two further methods of assassination. In one, the victim falls from a balcony. The 2018 death of the investigative journalist Maksim Borodin, who was exploring the extent of Russian military presence in Ukraine, was recorded as 'falling in accident from a balcony' (pp. 242-243). A few days before he had told a friend that he had seen someone with a weapon on his balcony and people in camouflage and masks on the shared landing. This method had been used by the KGB in 2007, when the journalist Ivan Safronov fell to his death from a fifth-floor flat. A pamphlet on assassinations prepared by the CIA in 1953, made available to the public in 1976, noted that a fall of 75 feet or more on to a hard surface was enough to kill anyone.

The second KGB method is the use of biological and chemical weapons. From the start of its nuclear programme in 1946 Russia produced polonium at its plant in Sarov; it has continued to do so although nuclear weapons no longer require that chemical. This was the poison used by two Russian agents to kill the exiled dissident writer and journalist Alexander Litvinenko in London in 2006. Another laboratory in the closed town of Shikhany developed a new class of nerve agents, Novichok (Newcomers), which were said to be eight times more powerful than VX, an earlier nerve gas. This was the poison, disguised in a perfume bottle, that was used in the plot to kill the Skripals in Salisbury in 2018. The Skripals were saved, but not Dawn Sturgess, who had sprayed herself with the 'perfume' after the bottle had been found by her boyfriend. In 1991 President Bush and President Gorbachev had signed the US-Soviet Chemical Weapons accord, stopping the production of and stockpiling of chemical weapons – so much for that!

The weakness of using poison for an assassination is that if it does not work and the victim survives, the plot unravels for the world to see.

Another new weapon was used by Kim Jung-un, the President of North Korea, in 2017 to assassinate his elder half-brother Kim Jung-nam when he was waiting for a flight in Kuala Lumpur Airport. He was attacked by two women: one sprayed a liquid on his face and the other covered his face with a cloth laced with a chemical. Within minutes he was unconscious and by the time he was taken to hospital he was dead. The two women, from Vietnam and Indonesia, were arrested the following day and claimed they had been told it was a prank. A post-mortem found traces on Kim's face of a VX nerve agent, banned under the Chemical Weapons Convention 1993 which North Korea had never ratified.

Protection from Attacks

It is very difficult to provide full security for MPs, since they have to meet their constituents face-to-face and openly go about their constituencies, so they are always vulnerable to deranged or vicious bigots. In 2000 Nigel Jones, the Lib Dem MP for Cheltenham, was attacked with a sword by a disgruntled constituent, Andrew Pennington; in 2010 Stephen Timms, a Labour MP, was stabbed and seriously wounded in a constituency surgery by a radical student; both were very lucky to survive these assassination attempts.

The security of the Prime Minister and other senior ministers – the Home Secretary, the Chancellor of the Exchequer and the Northern Ireland Secretary – has been significantly increased: gates are in place across the entrance to Downing Street, they have police protection at their homes, and two bodyguards in two bullet-proof cars when travelling, since that provides an opportunity for assassination. An attempt by the IRA in 1987 to kill Tom King, the Northern Ireland Secretary, in the garden of his house was foiled. Margaret Thatcher always travelled by car, never by train. When I asked her why, she said: 'If I travelled by train and the public got to know where I was going, security would have to be stepped up at all the stations at which we stopped and each bridge the train went under would have to be checked.' At least that was the advice she had received.

When the Soviet leader Mikhail Gorbachev and his wife visited London in 1984 it fell to me as the Education Secretary to look after Mrs Gorbachev while her husband was meeting the Prime Minister. We travelled to museums, cathedrals and schools in a bullet- and bomb-proof car that had been flown over from Russia, along with armed Soviet agents. I was quite glad to see the end of the security I had been given when I became Home Secretary, but others liked to cling on to the protection, no one more tenaciously than Ted Heath, who managed to hang on to his two Special Branch guards long after anyone was likely to threaten him.

Since President Kennedy was assassinated while travelling in an open-topped car no president has been allowed to do that again, or to stand up in a motorcade, presenting an easy target for a sniper. Security for a leading figure needs to be maintained at all times. I was surprised to find that some had been subject to several assassination attempts: Nkrumah of Nigeria faced five attempts and De Gaulle thirty-one. King Zog of Albania faced fifty-one, but in 1931 he decided to fight back. As he left the Opera House in Vienna in full evening dress two disgruntled officers fired at him: Zog pushed the body of his shot ADC aside, seized his revolver, and fired at the assassins who were captured.

Discreet teams of well-trained officers surround world leaders. In 2018 the Government of India announced that a team protecting President Modi consisted of thirty-six female counter-terrorists trained for fifteen months in explosives, urban warfare, and the deadly martial art of Krav Maga. The latter, pioneered by Israeli special forces, is a combination of boxing, wrestling, aikido, judo and karate. Even in London today this cult has at least eighteen training centres. The knowledge of such a trained team will, it is hoped, deter the amateur lone assassin seeking a lucky opportunity.

Verbal assassinations

I also considered whether the career or life of a public figure had been brought to an end as the result of a great speech, for given the moment a verbal assassination can be very effective. The most famous was Mark Antony's brilliant speech at Caesar's funeral which turned the crowd of Roman citizens against Brutus, the leader of the assassins, and made him an outcast. Two years later he was defeated by Caesar's nephew and he fell upon his sword.

There were three speeches in recent British history that precipitated the downfall of three Prime Ministers. The first was in the House of Commons debate on the Conduct of the War held on 7 and 8 May 1940. In April 1940 a British and French expeditionary Naval force had been sent to Norway to help Norwegians resist the invasion of their country by the Nazis. (The British Government was concerned that a German occupied Norway would give them a base closer to the UK for bombing raids.) The operation was a total failure and the Prime Minister, Neville Chamberlain, began the debate by reporting to the House that all the British troops and ships had been safely returned to Britain. Then the debate turned to the strong criticism of his faltering and hesitating leadership during the previous eight months. Lloyd George, Britain's Prime Minister during the First World War, ended his speech with "I say solemnly that the Prime Minister should give an example of sacrifice, because there is nothing which could contribute more to victory in this war, that he should sacrifice the seals of office." That was severe enough, but the devastating speech came from Leo Amery, a senior Conservative ex-Cabinet Minister (he had been the Secretary of State for India). He called upon Chamberlain to resign using Oliver Cromwell's words to the Long Parliament:

"… You have sat too long here for any good you have been doing. Depart I say and let us have done with you. In the name of God, go!"

In the vote the Conservative majority fell from 200 to 81, with 38 Tory MPs voting against the Government and 25 abstaining. On the following day, after Clement Attlee, the leader of the Labour Party, said he would not join a National Government led by Chamberlain, the Prime Minister resigned and advised the King to call on Churchill. A crucial debate that was very bitter. I remember John Profumo saying that as a serving officer he had turned up in uniform and spoke against the Prime Minister and, as he left the lobby some MPs spat on his shoes.

The second was in a debate in the House of Commons on the Profumo Affair on 17 June 1963 when Sir Nigel Birch, a tall, stooping, aristocratic MP took his revenge on Harold Macmillan. In 1958 Birch had resigned from the Treasury, together with the Chancellor of the Exchequer, Peter Thorneycroft, and Enoch Powell, the complete Treasury ministerial team, as Macmillan would not let them cut public expenditure. This should have created a crisis, but the Prime Minister immediately appointed another Chancellor and coolly departed on the same day for a visit to Russia dismissing it as "a little local difficulty."

British politics for the first six months of 1963 was dominated by the Profumo Affair. John Profumo, the Secretary of State for War, was rumoured to have had an affair with a beautiful call-girl, Christine Keeler, which he was forced to deny in a statement to the House of Commons. Unfortunately, the Russian Naval Attaché Avanov, a drunk, a womaniser and a spy from GRU, had also enjoyed her favours, opening up the possibility of a real security risk. The whole nation was gripped by the scandal: a ravishing beauty, a philandering minister with a beautiful actress wife, a Russian spy and a pimp who committed suicide. Eventually Profumo was forced to admit that he had lied to the House of Commons. Macmillan had been remarkably detached from all of this. In his diary he referred to "endless gossip", but he never spoke to Profumo to make his own judgement and was probably more indulgent since he was being cuckolded by his wife having a long affair with Bob Boothby MP. Harold Wilson, the Leader of the Opposition, had said, "The Prime Minister was gambling on the issue never seeing the light of day". In June the House called the Prime Minister to account and Birch chose his moment, scornfully attacking Macmillan's naivety about sex with "What is a whore about?" and finally using Browning's poem on William Wordsworth, The Lost Leader, as his weapon:

> . . . Let him never come back to us!
> There would be doubt, hesitation and pain.
> Forced praise on our part – the glimmer of twilight,
> Never glad confident morning again!

Macmillan crestfallen, bowed and dispirited, slunk out of the Chamber. Seventeen Tory MPs abstained and there were cries of "Resign!". When he went into the Smoking Room after the debate there were no Cabinet Ministers with him and only his son, Maurice, and son-in-law, Julian Amery, spoke to him. His premiership had come to an end and he was out of No.10 in October.

The third verbal assassination was Geoffrey Howe's resignation speech made on 13 November 1990 to a packed House of Commons. It lasted just ten minutes, but it was devastating. I was then the Conservative Party Chairman and following a successful Party Conference my task was to get Margaret Thatcher through the rest of the year and in particular to prevent any leadership challenge emerging before 15 November, the last date set by the 1922 Committee. That was not to be, as Geoffrey Howe, following Margaret's statement when she said, "No. No. No." to greater European integration, had had enough and resigned as Deputy Prime Minister on 1 November. This opened up the possibility of a leadership election and his speech twelve days later made it inevitable.

The House was packed and Geoffrey, flanked by Nigel Lawson who had resigned as Chancellor, and Michael Heseltine, set out with contained passion why he disagreed with her on the whole European issue and how officials and ministers were undermined by her interventions. On the night before, Margaret Thatcher at the Lord Mayor's Dinner had used a cricketing metaphor and boasted of her capacity to hit any ball out of the ground. Geoffrey, with a dry wit, said that Margaret's wrecking tactics on Europe were "rather like sending your opening batsmen to the crease only for them to find, at the moment the first ball is bowled, that their bats had been broken before the game by the team captain." He continued by saying that he had tried to express his feelings in the Cabinet, but he had failed to persuade her to be more moderate. His final words opened the door to an election – "The time has come for others to consider their own response to the tragic conflict of loyalties with which I have myself wrestled for perhaps too long." On the following day, 14 November Michael Heseltine announced his candidacy for the leadership, although he was not to win it. Throughout Geoffrey's speech, I was sitting next to Margaret on the front bench and she said to me, "I never thought that he would do it." In a later television programme Margaret did refer to "my assassination" by Geoffrey. He was one of the most gentle assassins in parliamentary history, but by far the most ruthlessly effective.

I

THE
UNITED KINGDOM
&
IRELAND

*'Assassination has never changed
the history of the world.'*

BENJAMIN DISRAELI, 1865

Assassination has been a rare event in the history of the United Kingdom. Over seven hundred years we have devised ways to resolve deeply held political and religious differences through a process of debate, discussion and negotiation underpinned by the toleration of dissenting views. It has been a long, slow process to establish the right of free expression; the right to hold protest meetings and marches; a press not controlled by the government of the day; no arbitrary arrest in the middle of the night; the development of the rule of law; corruption-free elections; the right to vote for everyone over the age of eighteen; and a recognition that opposition to the government in power is not a disloyal act.

Assassination has not played a part in transferring power from one person to another as was the practice in the Roman Empire and several European countries. There have however been suspicions. William Rufus in 1100 was found dead in a forest after hunting, killed by an arrow – accident or murder we will never know for sure, though most historians have opted for murder on the orders of his brother, who became Henry I.

The most famous assassination in the whole history of Britain occurred on 29 December 1170, when four knights, prompted by Henry II's rhetorical outburst, 'Who will rid me of this turbulent priest?', smashed Archbishop Becket's skull open on the steps of the altar in Canterbury Cathedral. This was a disastrously unsuccessful assassination, for it created a martyr who became a saint, and Henry II had to pay penance by prostrating himself before Becket's tomb and allowing monks to lash his back. This was definitely a poisoned chalice. Opposed to Becket, Henry wanted Common Law to prevail over Canon Law. He lost, and that had to await its resolution by Henry VIII four centuries later.

The assassination of Becket

Edward II (d. 1327) and Richard II (d. 1400) were prisoners after their defeat in battle and were almost certainly murdered to prevent them becoming rallying points for rebels. Henry VI (d. 1471), a prisoner in the Tower of London after the defeat of the Lancastrians and the death of his son Edward in the final battle of the Wars of the Roses at Tewkesbury, was murdered almost certainly by the command of Edward IV. Edward V in 1483 succeeded his father, but he and his brother Richard were immediately imprisoned in the Tower of London and murdered there. The assassin was their uncle, Richard III, though some have argued it may have been Henry Tudor. Shakespeare was in no doubt. His Richard III declares:

> Shall I be plain? – I wish the bastards dead
> And I would have it suddenly performed.

Several of our monarchs have been threatened, but none directly assassinated. Elizabeth I was the target of three Catholic plots – Rudolfi in 1571, Throckmorton in 1583, and Babington in 1586. Each of these promised an invasion by a Spanish army provided by Philip II and the assassination of the Queen, but the plotters never got anywhere near her: they were thwarted by the extensive network of spies – a prototype of MI5 and MI6 – built up by her spymaster, Sir Francis Walsingham. The plot with the most serious consequence was Babington's. It arose in the north and an assassin was identified: a former soldier, John Savage. The details of the plot were divulged to a Catholic, Gilbert Clifford, who was one of Walsingham's double agents. That led to the plot being nipped in the bud. Several of the plotters were hanged, drawn and quartered.

Walsingham used this plot as an opportunity to ensnare Mary, Queen of Scots, of whom he said: 'So long as that devilish woman lives neither Her Majesty must make an account to continue in quiet possession of the crown, nor her faithful servants assure themselves of safety for their lives.' Mary had known all the details of the plot to assassinate Elizabeth and had given it her approval: 'Let the great plot commence.' Walsingham arranged for all

Sir Francis Walsingham, Britain's first spymaster

the plotters' correspondence to Mary, which was coded and sent by being inserted in the stopper of a beer barrel, to be read by his agents. This proved to be her death warrant. In October Mary was sent to Fotheringhay Castle in Northamptonshire to be tried and condemned to death. What started as a plot to assassinate Elizabeth became a plot to assassinate Mary, Queen of Scots.

Elizabeth's ministers did not respond by trying to assassinate the Catholics who threatened her life: Jesuits and Catholic priests were treated to the due process of law – arrested, tortured, tried and executed.

Elizabeth's successor, James I, was a target for Catholic assassins who planned to kill him in the Gunpowder Plot of 1605. They had hoped that as the son of Mary, Queen of Scots, he would relax the harsh anti-Catholic laws, but very early on he made it clear that Catholics were not to increase their number and strength in his kingdom, and in 1604 Catholics and Jesuit priests were ordered to leave the country. Robert Catesby, a Yorkshire Catholic, with twelve other plotters planned to kill the King when he was making a speech to the two Houses of Parliament. In this case it was not the spying network that revealed the plot. One of the plotters wrote an anonymous letter to a friend, Lord Mounteagle, advising him to stay away from the opening of Parliament as 'they will receive a terrible blow this Parliament'. Every schoolboy and girl knows what happened next. On searching the Parliamentary cellars Guy Fawkes, a soldier who had fought for the Spanish, was found standing beside 36 barrels of gunpowder covered by some firewood. He was booted and spurred, prepared to escape after he had lit the fuse. Fawkes was not burnt at the stake: he was hanged, drawn and quartered in Old Palace Yard in January 1606. The consequence of this plot was that harsher laws against Catholics were quickly passed, so this assassination was a poisoned chalice for the Catholics.

The only successful assassination of a leading figure in the seventeenth century took place in 1628, when George Villiers, Duke of Buckingham, was killed. He had been a favourite of James I, rising rapidly from King's Master of Horse to become a viscount, a knight of the garter, an earl, and in 1623 a duke – the first duke to be created for a century. He became a close friend and a confidant of the new King Charles I, who appointed him as Lord Admiral. Charles's first Parliament in 1626 resented Villiers' influence and prepared his impeachment. He was saved then by Charles dissolving Parliament, but in 1628 the second Parliament returned to the attack.

On 22 August 1628, when Charles and Buckingham were in Portsmouth to arrange the victualling of the fleet, Villiers was surrounded by officials, and one stepped forward and plunged a dagger into his left breast. John Felton, a member of the minor gentry of Suffolk, had no political motive: as a soldier he bore a grudge that he had not been promoted to captain and that delays in pay had left him in debt. This is the sort of assassination that cannot be foreseen or prevented. Charles lost his strongest supporter, who could have stood between King and Parliament, but Villiers would not have been able to prevent the Civil War.

Oliver Cromwell
1656

Oliver Cromwell was a target for assassination after he had dissolved Parliament and assumed the role of Lord Protector of England, Scotland and Ireland in 1653. He resorted to running the country through twelve major generals, and although he declined the offer to be king he had all the trappings of kingship.

A disgruntled soldier, Edward Sexby, had fled to Flanders and there he planned various plots. He provided money to a disappointed Leveller, Miles Sindercombe, to organise a group to shoot Cromwell as he crossed Hyde Park or when he left Westminster Abbey. They never fired a shot, because they could not be sure of escaping. But they discovered that Cromwell had the habit of leaving central London on a Friday afternoon to enjoy the cleaner air of Hampton Court. They planned to ambush him as he passed through the congested streets of West London, but on the day he did not turn up. Then Sindercombe tried to set fire to Whitehall Palace where Cromwell lived by setting off a bomb in the chapel. One of his team betrayed him. He was condemned to be hanged, drawn and quartered, but he committed suicide in prison the night before his execution.

Sexby proclaimed him a martyr to 'the good old cause'.

In 1657 Sexby published a pamphlet that he may have written entitled *Killing No Murder*, which argued that it was lawful to kill a tyrant, quoting support from Aristotle, Cicero, the Bible and Machiavelli. It urged citizens to assassinate Cromwell: 'To us it particularly belongs to bring this Minister to justice.' Cromwell's spymaster John Thurloe was kept very busy and thwarted several other plots. Cromwell, keenly aware of his own security, never spent more than two nights in the same place.

Britain's first targeted killing: Napoleon
24 December 1800

I had always thought that in its history Britain had not engaged in the targeted killing of the head of its leading enemy, but as a result of the scrupulous research by Tim Clayton displayed in his recent book, *This Dark Business: The Secret War Against Napoleon*, I discovered that Britain was involved in an attempt to assassinate Napoleon in 1800.

A group of Breton Royalist officers called 'Chouans', led by ex-General Georges Cadoudal, were determined to kill Napoleon, the First Consul, and restore the Bourbons. Cadoudal flitted between London and Paris, usually on a cutter supplied by the Royal Navy. In April 1800 he fled to London and William Pitt, the Prime Minister, was advised of his presence by the War Secretary William Windham. In July Cadoudal, with another ex-general, had an interview with Pitt: Windham recorded that they told him 'Bonaparte would be cut-off before two months', but no countenance was given to it by the Prime Minister. However, the Government continued to supply the plotters with weapons and English gold which were regularly sent to France, and that was embarrassingly revealed when one gold consignment was misdirected. In the first six months of 1800 William Wickham, the agent of Foreign Secretary Grenville, spent significant sums on secret service expenditure, agents and various French soldiers. The British Cabinet may well not have endorsed the assassination attempt, but it funded and promoted its execution.

EXPLOSION D'UNE MACHINE INFERNALE

Failed attempt to assassinate Napoleon in Paris

In November 1800 Cadoudal sent two assassins to Paris with the specific task of killing Napoleon. They were Pierre de Saint-Régéant, a naval explosives expert, and Joseph de Limoëlan, an ex-officer whose father had been guillotined. The papers of William Windham reveal a list of persons including Saint-Régéant who received from the British Government 'an allowance for their services on the coast of France paid at the senior officer rate of 3 shillings a day'. In Paris they were helped by another conspirator, Carbon, who bought an old cart, a horse and an iron barrel and put into it a 200lb bomb and sharp stones, covered with hay. On 24 December they discovered that Napoleon was going to attend the first performance in France of Haydn's Creation in the Opera House, to celebrate the new libretto which had been written by Louis Philippe, Comte de Segur, who was to be Napoleon's Master of Ceremonies. They placed the cart and horse near some stone blocks to obstruct the rue Saint-Nicaise that Napoleon was bound to take. One of his grenadier outriders cleared a passage through the street, accidentally knocking Saint-Régéant to the ground; Napoleon's coach-driver whipped his horse to pass through quickly, and then took a sharp right turn. Saint-Régéant had lit the fuse of the bomb too late, and although Napoleon's coach was tipped on to one wheel it quickly recovered its balance. The explosion killed eight people and forty-five houses were reduced to rubble. Once Napoleon had ensured that Josephine's coach was safe, as she was travelling after him, he was greeted with cheers at the Opera House, and declared: 'Those bastards tried to blow me up. Have someone bring me the libretto of Haydn's Creation.'

Fouché, the Head of Police, blamed 'English gold', although initially Napoleon thought the attackers were Jacobins. His officers soon tracked down Carbon who had bought the cart; that led them to arrest Saint-Régéant, and both were guillotined in April. De Limoëlan managed to escape to the United States. If Napoleon had been killed the history of the world would have been different. For the Royalist plotters it was a poisoned chalice.

Spencer Perceval
11 May 1812

The only prime minister to be assassinated in our history was Spencer Perceval. He had served as Solicitor General, Attorney General and Chancellor of the Exchequer before becoming Prime Minister in 1809. He was a grey figure lacking any charisma, known as 'Little P' (for he was only 5 ft 4 in), whose main role was to raise sufficient money to fund Wellington's campaign in Portugal against Napoleon which was not going very well. His taxes bore heavily upon the people and there was widespread poverty and unrest.

On the sunny afternoon of 11 May 1812, as he entered the lobby of the House of Commons, a man who had been sitting near the fireplace rose, took a pistol out of his pocket, and shot Perceval in the chest. As he fell he cried out 'I am murdered'.

At first it was thought Perceval might have been the target of a political

Jⁿ. BELLINGHAM shooting the Right Hon SPENCER PERCEVAL.

The assassination of Spencer Perceval

protest against the war, but his assassin, John Bellingham, was simply an aggrieved citizen who had been imprisoned in Russia for four years over a debt and resented the fact that the British Government had done nothing to help him. When questioned he said: 'I have been denied the redress of many grievances by governments. I have been ill-treated. They all know who I am and what I am ... I am the most unfortunate man and feel here ... sufficient justification for what I have done.'

Bellingham's trial took place immediately at the Old Bailey and the jury were only out for fifteen minutes. It was intended that he should be taken to Newgate Prison, but a crowd had gathered outside trying to rescue him, as they welcomed the death of Little P. Later he was taken to Newgate guarded by soldiers. His lawyers entered a plea of insanity; this was rejected, and he was hanged just seven days after the murder, in spite of Lord Brougham and other lawyers protesting very strongly at the speed of the process. Bellingham's body was taken to St Bartholomew's Hospital, and among its collection of anatomical items for medical students you can still see Bellingham's skull.

The House of Commons had voted at once for a memorial in Westminster Abbey and a grant to Perceval's wife and six children of £50,000 (today's value is £2 million) and an annuity of £2,000.

This assassination did not create a political crisis. Lord Liverpool was immediately appointed as Perceval's successor and was to remain in office for fifteen years.

The Cato Street Conspiracy
23 February 1820

There were two attempts to blow up the Cabinet: the first was the Cato Street Conspiracy in 1820 and the second was the attempt on Margaret Thatcher's Cabinet at the Brighton Party Conference in 1984.

The first was led by a revolutionary radical, Arthur Thistlewood. He managed to attract twenty-seven supporters who rented a small building in Cato Street, just off the Edgware Road in London, which usefully had a hay loft. The plotters brought with them pistols and swords. However one of them, George Edwards, was a government spy: he passed the information to the Home Secretary, Sidmouth, who ordered that some Coldstream Guardsmen should work with the Bow Street police to stop this conspiracy. It was a complete set-up by the Home Office: they released the misinformation that the Cabinet was going to meet in Lord Harrowby's house in Grosvenor Square on 23 February. The plotters didn't bother to check the house – if they had, they would have seen that it was shut up. Cato Street had been under police surveillance. By 7.30pm the police thought that enough plotters had arrived for them to move in, and they found the conspirators meeting in the hay loft. The plotters were caught completely by surprise and did not even have time to fire their pistols, but Thistlewood drew his sword and killed one of the police officers, Richard Smithers.

The Cato Street conspirators resisting the police

Most of the conspirators were hanged in public; five were sentenced to deportation. These would-be assassins believed naively that following the death of most of the Cabinet there would be a general uprising, but they had made no preparations for that. It was a last-minute, botched-up operation, betrayed by a spy, that was doomed to fail. The Conservative Government survived for a further ten years.

Queen Victoria
1840–82 Assassination Attempts

There were seven assassination attempts on Queen Victoria, all carried out by single men who realised she was vulnerable when travelling in one of her carriages. The first was on 1 June 1840, when Edward Oxford, an eighteen-year-old unemployed pot boy, fired two shots from two pistols at the Queen as she was driving with Prince Albert in a phaeton, an open horse-drawn carriage, down Constitution Hill. He was insane. He said the two pistols were not loaded with bullets, and certainly none was found: they just had gunpowder in them.

The second attempt was in May 1842, again on Constitution Hill, when John Francis fired two shots. He was sentenced to death, but this was commuted to transportation. The third attempt was on 3 July 1842, by John Bean, a seventeen-year-old with a spinal injury that made him only four feet tall. He tried to fire two shots but his pistol failed to go off. It was found to have more tobacco than gunpowder in it. The fourth was on 19 May 1849: William Hamilton, an unemployed Irish bricklayer, fired from the same spot on Constitution Hill that Oxford had chosen, but his pistol too was only loaded with gunpowder. He said he did it with 'the purpose of getting into prison' as he was tired of being out of work. He was sent to prison in Gibraltar for seven years.

The fifth was on 27 May 1850 when an ex-officer, Robert Pate, a lunatic, struck Victoria on her forehead with his cane when her carriage was held up at a gate into Hyde Park. She stood up in the carriage and said, 'I am not hurt', but she was left with a black eye and a small scar. The sixth was on 29 February 1872 when a seventeen-year-old Irishman, Arthur O'Connor, climbed into the gardens of Buckingham Palace and got as close as one foot away from the Queen before he was thrown to the ground by the Queen's personal servant, John Brown.

The seventh and last took place on 7 March 1882, when Roderick Maclean fired a pistol at the Queen as she was leaving Windsor Station. She wrote: 'There was a sound of what I thought was an explosion from the engine, but in a moment, I saw people rushing about and a man being hustled rushing down the street.' He was tried for treason, found 'not guilty, but insane', and committed to Broadmoor.

The Queen was clearly at risk when she was travelling in a carriage, and it is extraordinary that neither the police nor the army were used to protect her. All her assassins were solitary deranged figures. After this last attempt she wrote to Gladstone, the Prime Minister, on 23 April insisting that the plea should be changed to 'guilty, but insane'.

GOD SAVED THE QUEEN!

This Accurate Representation of
EDWARD OXFORD SHOOTING AT THE QUEEN,
on being held before a Strong Light, MAGICALLY discovers the means which
SAVED OLD ENGLAND'S HOPE FROM THE ASSASSIN'S AIM!!
(Designed by the Great Wizard!)

The first attempted assassination of Queen Victoria

Punishment deters not only sane men but also eccentric men, whose supposed involuntary acts are really produced by a diseased brain capable of being acted upon by external influence. A knowledge that they would be protected by an acquittal on the grounds of insanity will encourage these men to commit desperate acts, while on the other hand certainty that they will not escape punishment will terrify them into a peaceful attitude towards others.

Victoria thought that if Edward Oxford had been hanged it would have deterred the other regicides – a highly doubtful proposition.

Her son Edward, just before he succeeded in 1900, was shot at on Brussels

Railway Station by a fifteen-year-old anarchist who got to within two yards of the Prince, but missed. Edward commented: 'If he had not been so bad a shot I don't see how he could have possibly missed me.'

Robert Peel
20 January 1843

One leading politician in the Victorian age had a very lucky escape. Robert Peel, the Prime Minister, was saved from an assassin's bullet because someone else was mistaken for him. Edward Drummond, who came from the Drummond banking family, had joined the Civil Service in 1814 and had become the secretary to four Conservative prime ministers: George Canning, Viscount Goderich, the Duke of Wellington and Robert Peel. On 20 January 1843 he left Peel's house in Whitehall Gardens at 4.00pm to walk to No. 10 Downing Street.

A mad Scotsman, Daniel McNaughton, son of a Glasgow woodturner, mistook him for the Prime Minister and shot him in the back. The bullet passed through his chest and lung and lodged in his abdomen and he died five days later. McNaughton's counsel pleaded insanity and three judges established what became known as the McNaughton Rule, namely that the key test for a jury was whether the accused was capable of distinguishing right from wrong in respect of his actions at the time he had acted. McNaughton was found to be insane.

If Peel had been assassinated that day it is likely that either Disraeli or Bentinck would have become prime minister. They would probably not have repealed the Corn Laws in 1845 which created Free Trade and was seen as the pillar on which Victorian prosperity was built.

Daniel McNaughton

IRELAND

Lord Frederick Charles Cavendish
6 May 1882

The assassination in Dublin of an English cabinet minister, Lord Frederick Cavendish, the Irish Secretary, had significant consequences.

Gladstone in 1882 was trying to reduce violence in Ireland by seeking a deal with the Irish MPs in Westminster, led by Charles Stewart Parnell, whom he released from Kilmainham Jail. Gladstone hoped to launch a new era of cooperation which would replace coercion and the eviction of tenants. The Irish Secretary Forster resigned as he did not agree with the release, and Gladstone replaced him with an able minister from his Government, Lord Frederick Cavendish. Cavendish's father, the Duke of Devonshire, advised him not to accept, as he was no orator and Irish politics needed oratory. In Dublin on 6 May, after he had taken the oath, he decided to accompany his deputy, Thomas Burke, who intended to walk home across Phoenix Park. This news had reached the ears of a group of terrorists known as the Invincibles. Armed with twelve-inch surgical knives bought in London and smuggled into Dublin under the skirts of the pregnant wife of the secretary of the Land League, they hacked both Cavendish and Burke to death.

Such was the public outrage at this murder that coercion was revived and the movement towards cooperation abandoned. Cavendish's murder also had a much wider influence on future events in Ireland. His elder brother, Lord Hartington (Secretary of State for India), was so appalled by the brutal murder that he decided to oppose the growing campaign for Home Rule for the whole of Ireland, which Gladstone was beginning to advocate. After the 1886 election Hartington declined to serve in Gladstone's Government as he could not support the Home Rule Bill. He left the Liberal Party to form the Liberal Unionist Party, which destroyed the Liberal majority in the House of Commons and

The assassination of Lord Frederick Cavendish and Thomas Burke in Phoenix Park

led to the Tories forming the next government, which Hartington joined. This split delayed the possibility of any settlement for twenty-eight years, until the Liberals had a large majority and introduced the third Home Rule Bill in 1914. That was overtaken by the First World War, and the idea of Home Rule was not revived after 1918.

This was another assassination that achieved exactly the reverse of what the assassins intended.

* * *

Acts of violence by terrorists continued throughout the province of Ulster and only came to an end with the Good Friday Agreement of 1998, when Sinn Fein was given a place in the Government of Ulster.

In the twentieth century most assassinations were not carried out by lunatics, aggrieved citizens or anarchists: they were planned and ruthlessly implemented by terrorist organisations. In the time of the Troubles in Ireland from 1968 to 1998 Catholic terrorists in both Eire and Ulster used assassination to try to create a united Ireland by joining the six counties in the north, Ulster, to the twenty-three counties in the south. To counter this, Protestant terrorists used assassination in Ulster. It was the first time in our history that the assassination of leading politicians, including the indiscriminate murder of many innocent citizens, was used as a political weapon. Once again the politics of Ireland exerted its powerful disruptive influence upon the politics of this island, and in the Brexit negotiations of 2018–19 the trading position of Ulster, known as the 'Backstop', became the central non-negotiable issue.

Michael Collins
22 April 1922

In the early twentieth century Michael Collins had been elected President of the Irish Supreme Council of the Irish Republican Brotherhood. In the campaign to free Ireland from British rule he had set up an assassination squad known as the 'Twelve Apostles' to kill government agents or police officers identified as being exceptionally hostile by spies whom he had placed in the government. Fourteen were assassinated. He was the leader of the movement that used violence to further its political aims.

However, this charismatic terrorist leader of the IRA was murdered in County Cork by IRA terrorists, who believed that he had betrayed Ireland by accepting the separation of Ulster, left a part of the United Kingdom. He had recognised that the Protestants in the north would never agree to a united Ireland, and in 1921 he led the negotiations with Lloyd George from the Irish side and agreed to a separate Ulster state. He knew how unpopular that would be, and on leaving the signing he said, 'I have signed my own death warrant.'

After the legislation was passed a civil war broke out between the new Irish Government forces led by Collins and the renegade IRA who would not give up. With the help of British weapons, Collins defeated the Republican forces in Dublin and Cork. He decided to visit Cork to see his troops and to open peace negotiations, although he was advised not to go, as the IRA were very active

"They'll never shoot me in my own country"

in the southern part of Ireland. On 22 April 1922 his convoy, consisting of one motorcyclist, his open touring car and an armed car, was ambushed on a small country road at Beal na mBlath near Clonakilty, forced to stop, and fired upon from the hills. Collins jumped out and fired back with a rifle but he was hit in the head.

The assassins hoped that by killing Collins they could shift the balance of the war in their favour. That did not happen. The Irish Free State won the war, and its Government remained in power for another nine years. Collins had won the respect of the British politicians with whom he had negotiated – Churchill and Lloyd George – and if he had lived longer he might have become a great Irish prime minister. He was just thirty-two years old, and he had shown that he was capable of modifying his earlier views. He was given a state funeral. Collins might have been able to establish a different future for Ireland, but it is one of the recurring tragedies in Irish history that when a major change is implemented that involves some degree of compromise, a small group of determined revolutionaries will not accept it and will want to continue the fight.

Sir Henry Wilson
22 June 1922

Two months after Collins' assassination, Sir Henry Wilson, a successful soldier in the First World War and a passionate advocate for an independent Protestant Ulster, who had become the Conservative MP for North Down in Ulster, was assassinated in London.

In his maiden speech on 14 March he had urged that the constabulary in Northern Ireland should be reformed, expanded and armed, creating in effect an armed force. On 22 June 1922, wearing full military uniform, he unveiled a war memorial at Liverpool Street Station and returned to his home at 36 Eaton Place around 2.30pm. As he was opening the door a bullet hit the wood; turning round and drawing his ceremonial sword he saw two men, who fired six more shots. His wife helped him inside but he died in the hallway.

The two Irish Catholic assassins, Reginald Dunn and Joseph O'Sullivan, ran off but did not get very far as one had a wooden leg. They were probably following the order of Michael Collins, who had earlier ordered Wilson's assassination. Both were found guilty. Dunn was not allowed to speak, as it would be a political speech justifying the right to kill, but he did have the last word: when the judge ended his death sentence with 'And may the Lord have mercy on your soul', Dunn shouted, 'He will, my Lord'. Justice was swift in those days and they were hanged on 10 August. This assassination had no effect at all upon the tragedy that was about to overwhelm Ireland: a civil war.

THE TROUBLES

On 5 October 1968 a civil rights march in Londonderry took place though banned. It led to clashes with the police, sparked widespread rioting across Northern Ireland, and led to thirty years of violent conflict that only came to an end with the Good Friday Agreement in 1998. In those thirty years 3,600 people were killed and many more seriously injured as the result of attacks in which many innocent bystanders were killed, and leading politicians became the victim of targeted killings.

Sir Hugh Fraser MP
23 October 1975

Sir Hugh Fraser luckily escaped assassination after a bomb had been placed under his car by the IRA when it was parked outside his house in London. It was accidentally exploded by Gordon Hamilton Fairley, a leading cancer specialist at St Bartholomew's Hospital, who was simply walking by: just before Fraser was about to approach his car Fairley was killed. Hugh Fraser was a vocal and fearless critic of IRA terrorism and had become a target. On that day in October 1975 Caroline Kennedy, daughter of the assassinated American President John F. Kennedy, was staying with the Frasers, and she too would have been killed if they had reached the car before Fairley. Several members of the IRA were tried in 1977 for this assassination and other bombings, including the assassination of Ross McWhirter, and given long sentences.

Sir Hugh Fraser's car outside his house after the explosion

'I live in constant fear of my life. I know that the IRA have got me on their death list.'

Ross McWhirter
27 November 1975

Ross and his brother Norris were sports journalists in the 1950s who used their extensive knowledge of sports and other subjects and their encyclopaedic memories to create The Guinness World Records, first published in 1955. In the 1960s Ross became an active supporter of the Conservative Party. I met him in 1970 when the St Marylebone Conservative Association was selecting a candidate for the by-election caused by the appointment of Quintin Hogg to be Lord Chancellor. The three final contestants were Douglas Hurd, Ross McWhirter and myself. He did not win, but I was told that he made a very impressive speech.

Ross advocated the return of the death penalty for terrorists. The IRA had

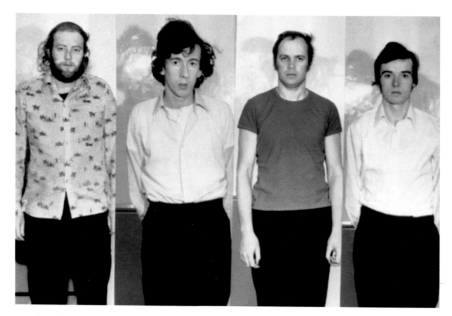

The four IRA murderers – Harry Duggan, Edward Butler, Hugh Doherty and Martin O'Connell

launched a fourteen-month bombing campaign in London, exploding forty bombs, killing thirty-five people and injuring many more, and Ross launched a 'Beat the Bombers' campaign in which he offered a £50,000 reward for information leading to the conviction of any IRA bomber. He did not stop there: he proposed that all Southern Irish nationals living in Britain should be registered with the local police and provide photographic ID of themselves when renting flats or booking into hotels. He knew the risk he was taking: 'I live in constant fear of my life. I know that the IRA have got me on their death list.' He was particularly incensed by the death of the cancer specialist Gordon Fairley, who happened to be walking past a parked car that belonged to the MP Hugh Fraser which had had a bomb placed under it by the IRA.

On 27 November 1975 two gunmen, Harry Duggan and Hugh Docherty, hid in the garden of his house in Enfield, north London. When they knew he was inside they knocked on his door and when he opened it they shot him dead.

The assassins turned out to be members of a murderous gang who had thrown a bomb through the window of the celebrated restaurant Scott's in Mount Street. Fortunately that did not hurt anybody, but the police had discovered that when a gang's attack was unsuccessful they often returned to the same place to try again; sure enough they did, but two police were keeping the restaurant under observation and when the second bomb was thrown they grabbed a passing taxi and followed the getaway car. The gang eventually took refuge in a council flat at 22 Balcombe Street, holding a couple as hostages. This siege was in my constituency, so I went to see how it was being handled by the police, led brilliantly by Police Commissioner Peter Imbert. They were determined not to lose any more lives, so they took six days to elicit surrender. The four IRA terrorists – Hugh Doherty, Martin O'Connell, Edward Butler and Harry Duggan – were convicted of murdering nine persons. They served twenty-three years in prison, but as part of the Good Friday Agreement in 1998 they were released, and welcomed by Gerry Adams as 'Our Nelson Mandelas'. I don't recall any incident when Nelson Mandela murdered innocent people.

Airey Neave DSO, MC, OBE, MP
30 March 1979

Airey Neave was murdered just two days after the General Election of 1979 had been announced. As forecasts pointed to a win for Margaret Thatcher, it was clear that Airey would become the Northern Ireland Secretary. Irish Republicans, whether IRA or INLA, looked upon him as their Number One Enemy. He was implacably opposed to a united Ireland and looked upon the IRA as criminals, rebels and traitors. Direct rule from London would be reinforced and there would be no move towards an elected assembly in Ulster. He simply had to be stopped.

He had had a remarkable career. In the Second World War he was captured in 1940, escaped, but was caught again and sent to Colditz, a prison from which no-one was expected to escape, but he did, and as he had fluent German he managed

Airey contemplating the next move

to reach Switzerland. After the war he served with the military tribunal at the Nuremburg Trials and was then recruited to be an agent of MI6. This gave Airey Neave the conspiratorial aura that served him well in politics.

As he was not a supporter of Edward Heath Airey did not get a ministerial post in 1970, which he might well have expected. After the Government's electoral defeat in February 1974 Airey bluntly told Heath that he should go as leader of the Conservative Party and thereafter plotted to bring him down. He tried to persuade Keith Joseph, Willie Whitelaw and even Edward du Cann to stand as leader, and when they declined he offered to be Margaret Thatcher's campaign manager. He ran her campaign brilliantly and formed a very strong personal friendship with Margaret, becoming manager of her private office and Shadow Northern Ireland Secretary.

On 30 March 1979 the Irish National Liberation Army – the political wing of the Marxist Republican Socialist Party which had made several attacks on the security forces and the British Army – decided to strike. This was because if Margaret Thatcher were to win Airey would become Northern Ireland Secretary and he was determined to root out Irish Republican terrorism. Two members of the INLA gained entry to the MPs' underground car park and fixed a magnetic car bomb, fitted with a ball-bearing switch, under the driver's seat of Airey Neave's new Vauxhall Cavalier. They used this ingenious bomb instead of a time bomb since they could not be sure when Airey would be in his car. As he drove up the ramp of the car park the bomb would be detonated.

I was in the library of the House of Commons at that time and the explosion was so loud I knew that something had happened very close to us. Looking out of the window I saw a car ripped apart on the slope coming up from the car park. A quarter of an hour later I saw Peter Thorne, the Serjeant at Arms, in his usual ceremonial dress, go down the ramp to confirm the identification of the driver. Airey was unconscious; one of his legs had been blown off below the knee and the other was just hanging on. He was to die shortly afterwards in hospital. The House of Commons in a very sombre mood began to fill up in almost complete silence and then Labour's Chief Whip said he had to report the tragic and appalling news that a Member had been killed. What a way to start a general election.

The IRA denied that they had perpetrated the crime. The actual culprits boasted: 'Airey Neave got a lot of his own medicine when an INLA unit pulled off the operation of the decade and blew him to bits inside the "impregnable" Palace of Westminster.'

Margaret Thatcher's response was: 'They must never, never, never be allowed to triumph. They must never prevail.'

As often occurs, various other claims were made as to who was guilty. One of the most extraordinary was from Enoch Powell, who argued that MI6 prompted by the Americans had carried out the deed, as America wanted a united Ireland.

My first reaction of shock and horror was quickly followed by amazement and fear that murderous terrorists had breached the security of the Palace of Westminster and might even have got into the Chamber. Immediately the checking of cars was tightened up; undercarriages were checked with mirrors

"Death of one of freedom's warriors", Margaret Thatcher

held on long rods; backs of vans were opened for inspection; and barriers were placed along the front of the Palace to prevent a frontal attack by a vehicle with a bomb inside. All of this did not stop a man armed with a knife breaking into the yard of the Palace in 2017 and stabbing a policeman to death. Following that there are now armed police officers at all entrances to the Palace, who also patrol around and in front of the building.

In 2019 the Home Secretary Sajid Javid asked the Metropolitan Police to re-open the investigation into Airey Neave's death. The Chief Whip of the Democratic Unionist Party had questioned why Harry Flynn, a former key member of the INLA, was living in Spain without having been 'pursued by authorities' in relation to the case.

Lord Louis Mountbatten
27 August 1979

'What would they want with an old man like me?'

Lord Mountbatten, a cousin of the Queen, had a spectacular career. He was Supreme Allied Commander in South East Asia from 1943 to 1946, the last Viceroy of India in 1947, and the first Governor General of India in 1947–8. From 1954 to 1959 he was the First Sea Lord, a position that his father had held forty years earlier, and was Chief of the Defence Staff from 1959 to 1965. He was also Chairman of the NATO Military Committee for one year.

He was very well known, easily recognised, at the centre of the establishment and close to the royal family, being a mentor to Charles, Prince of Wales. He spent much of each summer at Cassiebann Castle in Mullaghmore, a small seaside village in County Sligo, just twelve miles south of the border with Northern Ireland. In 1978 the IRA allegedly had tried to shoot him on his boat, but choppy water stymied the sniper.

On 27 August 1979 Mountbatten planned to pick up some lobster pots from his fishing yacht, *Shadow V*, and he had invited some of his family to join him – his daughter Patricia (Lady Brabourne) and her husband John, a film director;

Happier days

their two sons, Nicholas and Timothy; and John's elderly mother Doreen. My
wife knew John Brabourne, as they were both directors of Thames Television.

When the boat was some two hundred yards away from the shore there was
a huge explosion. A bomb had been detonated, destroying the boat and killing
Mountbatten, his fourteen-year-old grandson Nicholas, and Paul Maxwell, a
local boatboy. The Dowager Lady Brabourne died the following day. A radio
fusebomb had been planted in the yacht's engine room by an IRA member,
Thomas McMahon, who was arrested within hours of the murder when his car
was stopped by the police at a routine Garda checkpoint. The driver, Francis
McGirl, was acquitted. But the forensic evidence of sand, green paint from
the boat on McMahon's boots and nitroglycerine on his clothes led to his life
imprisonment.

The Provisional IRA claimed credit. This was Gerry Adams' twisted logic:

'What the IRA did to Mountbatten is what he had been doing all his life to other people . . . with his own record I don't think he could have objected to dying in what was clearly a war situation.'

It emerged later that the Provos had set up an assassination team a few months before, possibly goaded to do so by INLA's success in assassinating Airey Neave the previous year.

Christopher Tugendhat
3 December 1980

When Christopher Tugendhat left Cambridge University he became a journalist, working for the *Financial Times* as features and leader writer. In 1970 he became the Conservative MP for the Cities of London and Westminster South. In the same year I was elected for the neighbouring seat of Marylebone and Westminster North, so we became close colleagues. In 1977 he was offered the post of European Commissioner by the Labour Prime Minister, James Callaghan. Instead of accepting the nominee of the Conservative leader, Margaret Thatcher, Callaghan had spotted Christopher's very strong support for the Common Market and his positive approach to Britain's membership of the European Community. Four years later Margaret Thatcher as Prime Minister reappointed him, and from 1981 to 1985 he was Vice-President of the Commission. The attempt to assassinate him occurred in December 1980. This is how he described it:

> It occurred as I was leaving our house in the Avenue de l'Hippodrome in Brussels. A car pulled up and a man leant out of the rear window and fired 3 bullets from an armalite that went into the door jamb beside and above me. The IRA claimed the attempt later that day. It was at the time when Mountbatten had been killed and also the British diplomat in The Hague or maybe that was bungled too. They wanted to show that no prominent Brit abroad was safe. I was a good target because, as I wasn't a servant of the Crown but of the Commission, nobody thought they

would have a go at me. I therefore didn't have any protection, unlike the 3 ambassadors in Brussels, and Roy Jenkins as an ex Home Secretary. It is thought I escaped for 2 reasons. One was that normally I was fetched by a driver, but on this occasion I had driven myself home the night before, as my driver was in a bowls competition, and the car was parked outside the house. My routine, therefore, was different from usual. The other was that I had just turned to speak to Julia over my shoulder and so probably veered at the last moment. One's immediate reaction is that such a thing couldn't have happened and to carry on as usual. So I drove into the office to report the matter as our telephone wasn't connected (we had only recently moved into the house) and Julia went to the hairdresser as we were lunching that day at the palace for the King's farewell to the Jenkins Commission. Thereafter I had wall to wall protection, bullet proof limo and all kinds of gizmos in the house.

Ian Gow MP
30 July 1990

'I am at less risk than any serving officer in Her Majesty's Ulster Constabulary.'

Ian Gow and I were friends for over twenty years, for our two houses in East Sussex were just five miles apart. He had fought two safe Labour seats in the elections of 1964 and 1966, but it was not until 1974 that he was returned for the safe Conservative seat of Eastbourne. The Dog House, an old farmhouse just north of Eastbourne, became his home with his wife Jane and their two boys. It was a house of happiness; whenever we visited them there was laughter and gossip, cricket and tennis.

In the House of Commons Ian struck up a close friendship with Airey Neave, and he was shattered by his assassination just before the 1979 election. By that time he had become part of Margaret's inner circle, and after her victory she appointed him her Parliamentary Private Secretary, a post he was to hold for four years. It was one of her best appointments: Ian, deeply loyal to her, was

Ian and Margaret

constantly at her side, a crony who could mull over with her what had happened that day with a glass of Famous Grouse. He spent many hours in the House of Commons talking to Tory Backbenchers, helping them to sort out their problems, identifying troublemakers as well as talented MPs who could be candidates for government jobs.

Ian had a very charming habit of inviting both difficult and ambitious MPs to have lunch with him at the Cavalry Club as he had served in the Hussars during his National Service. Lunch with Ian always started with a White Lady. I joined him on several occasions, for I was supposed at that time to be a Heathite. It is now forgotten how very unpopular Margaret Thatcher was in 1980 and 1981: these were years of severe economic depression with high unemployment, high inflation, and many companies closing down every day. In this political crisis Ian Gow did a great deal to steady the ship. By nature he was an optimist, and even in those dark political days he found it possible to be cheerful.

In 1983 Margaret felt he should be rewarded by becoming a minister. However when in 1985 she signed the Anglo-Irish Agreement that was to lead to an assembly in Northern Ireland with the support of the Irish Government, he resigned. Ian made it clear in his resignation speech that he remained loyal to Margaret – 'The first Chief, the most resolute leader and the kindest friend'. As Chairman of the Northern Ireland Tory Backbench Committee he redoubled his support for Northern Ireland, opposing power-sharing and drawing closer to Enoch Powell and Ian Paisley.

On 30 July 1990 at 8.39am he got into his Austin Montego car which was parked outside his house. He did not think it was necessary to check the underside: if he had he would have seen the 4.5lb bomb. When he reversed his car in the drive the bomb was detonated, the car was blown apart, and Ian was killed.

Ian had been very casual about his own security. An IRA assassination list was discovered in December 1988 and not surprisingly his name was on it. In the 1980s ministers were advised to check their cars carefully: we were given a stick with a mirror attached so that we could search underneath to see if a bomb

Killed in his car

had been attached. If Ian had done that he would not have been killed. Some weeks earlier at a party Jonathan Aitken had chided him to take more care of his security: 'Ian, old lad, I hope you vary your route to the Commons and check under your car.' Ian replied: 'Certainly not. I am at less risk than any serving officer in Her Majesty's Ulster Constabulary, and anyway I wouldn't know what to look for.' Ian's widow Jane has claimed that the two IRA murderers were known to the police, but their names have not been revealed.

He died just a few months before Margaret Thatcher had to face a leadership election, so he was not around when she needed him most. In that election her current Parliamentary Private Secretary was absolutely useless. She needed just four more votes to secure her victory, and I am sure that if Ian had been around he would have persuaded even more than four Backbenchers to support her.

Tony Berry, Roberta Wakeham and three other Conservatives 12 October 1984

The IRA planned to kill the Prime Minister, Margaret Thatcher, during the Conservative Party Conference in Brighton in October 1984 by placing a bomb in the Grand Hotel where she and other politicians were staying. It was detonated at 2.54am on 12 October. Mary and I were at the Conference, but we had to return to London in the early morning: as Minister for Local Government I had a breakfast TV debate with the Mayor of London, Ken Livingstone, as I was carrying a Bill through Parliament to abolish the Greater London Council (I had planned a series of debates between 'Red Ken' and 'Blue Ken'). We left the hotel around 1.30am and met Tony Berry, Deputy Chief Whip, who had been taking his small dog for a walk on the promenade. Less than two hours later he was dead.

Sir Anthony came from the Berry journalist family and was delightful, very popular, tall and elegant, a natural Whip. We had got to know each other very well, and he was my regular bridge partner. He had promoted my chances: at the end of 1980 he had arranged for Margaret Thatcher, after a day of campaigning

in Surrey, to drop into our house in my Dorking constituency for tea. She sat in an easy chair in our conservatory looking out on the garden. Mary had placed on a table beside her a small bowl of freshly picked sweet black gooseberries, all of which Margaret devoured. Whether it was Tony's advice or the gooseberries, shortly afterwards she asked me to join her Government as the Minister for Information Technology.

The bomb also killed four other people: Roberta Wakeham, the wife of John, the

Tony Berry

The assassin

Chief Whip; Jeanne Chattock, the wife of the Conservative Chairman in the West of England; Eric Taylor, a local party official; and Lady Maclean, wife of the President of the Scottish Conservatives. Thirty-one others were injured.

The bomb had been placed under the bath in Room 269, one floor above the Thatchers' suite, and it had a long delay timer. When it exploded it brought down a tall central chimney which caused most of the damage. Margaret had a lucky escape, as she had just left her bathroom a few minutes before the bomb exploded: the bathroom was destroyed, but her sitting room and bedroom were unscathed. The debris crashed down through John Wakeham's room and carried him down to the ground floor; he was only saved by a large beam that stopped more of the hotel collapsing on top of him. The rescuers took seven hours to reach him, tunnelling alongside to avoid the beam falling on him.

Norman Tebbit was also carried down by the debris. He was not rescued for four hours, and his slow descent strapped to a stretcher in front of the wrecked

On the way to the police station

hotel was captured by TV. When asked by one of the medical staff if he was allergic to anything he replied, 'Yes. Bombs.' His wife Margaret, permanently disabled in the attack, had to spend two years in hospitals, and Norman devoted the rest of his life to caring for her.

Immediately the IRA claimed responsibility for the attempted assassination of 'Thatcher the Warmonger', and chillingly said: 'Today we were unlucky. Remember we only have to be lucky once.' The man who planted the long delay time bomb of 20lb of gelignite was an IRA member, Patrick Magee, who had stayed at the hotel under the name of Roy Welsh over the weekend of 14–15

September. He was tracked down and sentenced to life imprisonment, but under the terms of the Good Friday Agreement he was released after serving fourteen years. He never repented.

Margaret and Denis were taken to the Brighton Police Station in their nightclothes. Alistair McAlpine, the Conservative Treasurer, had the good sense to get the Marks & Spencer store in Brighton to open early so that the people affected could buy new clothes.

When she left the station Margaret asserted that the Tory Conference would go on. Defiant and determined not to let the IRA win, she told the Party workers:

> We suffered a tragedy not one of us could have thought would happen in our country. We picked ourselves up and sorted ourselves out, as all good British people do. I thought let us stand together for we are British. The IRA was trying to destroy the fundamental freedom that is the birthright of every British citizen: freedom, justice and democracy.

For her it was a Churchillian moment, and her popularity soared to the levels it had reached in the Falklands War.

If Margaret had been killed in 1984 the Tory MPs would have had to choose a new leader. The choice would have been between Geoffrey Howe and Michael Heseltine, both convinced Europeans. At that time the Eurosceptic movement in the Conservative Party was restricted to a handful of MPs; only much later did the Party turn against Europe, led by a speech that Margaret made in Bruges in 1988. It was certain that any new leader would not have embraced Euroscepticism, and Britain would have remained firmly in the Common Market and the European Union. It is even possible that the Labour Party, which had campaigned in the 1983 election to come out of Europe, would have become the Eurosceptic party. If that had happened there would probably never have been a referendum on membership of the EU. Idle speculation, but it might have turned out that way. By surviving the assassination attempt, it could be said that Margaret Thatcher was able to pave the way for Britain's departure from the European Union.

TWO POLITICIANS ASSASSINATED, NOT BY THE IRA
Richard Sharples
10 March 1973

Sir Richard Sharples, a Conservative MP from 1954 to 1972, was a close friend of Ted Heath (he taught him to sail). When Heath won the 1970 election he appointed Dick as Minister of State in the Home Office. I had joined the Government in 1971 as a junior minister for the Civil Service Department which was the Prime Minister's department, so I met Dick with Ted on several occasions.

In 1972 Dick resigned to take up the post of Governor of Bermuda. After a dinner party in his house in Hamilton on 10 March 1973 he decided to take a stroll in the garden with his ADC, Captain Hugh Sayers. They were ambushed and shot. There was a massive search by police, but it was not until three years later, in 1976, that a petty criminal called Erskine Burrows was arrested. He confessed to killing them both – and also confessed to killing the Bermudian Police Commissioner in 1972. It emerged that he was a member of a revolutionary black nationalist organisation, the Black Beret Cadre. In his confession he wrote:

> The motive for killing the Governor was to seek to make the people, black people in particular, become aware of the evilness and wickedness of the colonialist system in this island. Second the motive was to show that these colonialists were just ordinary people like ourselves who eat, sleep and die just like anybody else, and we must not stand in fear and awe of them.

Another Black Beret, Larry Tacklyn, was acquitted as an accomplice, but charged with another murder. They were both found guilty. After an appeal to the House of Lords they were hanged in 1977, though there had been a moratorium on executions since 1945. They were the last two people to be executed under British rule anywhere in the world.

The Governor and his ADC

At the time of the assassination I was the minister who policed the service contracts of public servants, and I was asked to consider whether Dick Sharples and Captain Sayers had been killed in the line of duty. It would have been advantageous to them both as regards pensions and death duties and I was sympathetic, but the Ministry of Defence ruled that they had not died on active service.

As a postscript, Dick's wife Pamela was made a life peer in 1977. She attended the House of Lords regularly, asking questions until her retirement in 2017.

If the purpose of Burrows was to precipitate the end of colonial rule in Bermuda, he failed. In 1995 there was a referendum to decide whether Bermuda should become an independent sovereign state or a British colony: 74 per cent voted against independence, since Bermuda had prospered as an international financial centre and that wealth had trickled down to many Bermudians.

Jo Cox MP
16 June 2016

In the election of 2015 Jo Cox won her first parliamentary seat in the safe Labour threshold of Batley and Spens, increasing the Labour majority. After leaving Cambridge she had worked as a political assistant to Glenys Kinnock in Europe and then moved to Oxfam, becoming head of policy, then head of humanitarian campaigns for Oxfam International in New York, where she did much work with disadvantaged groups in the Third World. This became one of her abiding interests as a Member of Parliament.

In her first year as an MP, which so tragically turned out to be her last, Jo Cox was incredibly active in campaigning for peace in Syria. She formed the first All Party Group of Friends for Syria. She also worked closely with the Conservative MP Tom Tugendhat on the Chilcot Report into the Iraq conflict. She was a committed and active MP, popular in the House, highly regarded, and clearly destined for ministerial office.

On 16 June 2016, in the middle of the referendum campaign in which she supported Remain, she went to hold a surgery for her constituents in Birstall. As she arrived she was shot three times, once in the head, and then stabbed several times, by a fifty-two-year-old constituent, Thomas Mair, who had a history of psychiatric problems and links with a neo-Nazi group in America. He had shouted out when he attacked her, 'Britain first.' She died four hours later. Mair was found guilty of murder and given a whole life tariff, never to be released from prison.

This was a terrible tragedy, made all the worse as she had two young children and a devoted husband. The country was horrified and shocked that such a good person at the start of her active political life should be killed doing her duty by serving her constituents and her country. A very bright light of the future had been brutally extinguished.

Jo Cox

Dealing with political terrorists

Throughout our history we had not resorted to targeted killing, but our engagement in the war against ISIL or ISIS (the Islamic State of Iraq and the Levant, also known as Daesh) led the British Government to use drones to kill British citizens who had left Britain to join our enemies as Islamic State fighters, then killed other British citizens, and could possibly have gone on to kill even more.

Reyaad Khan, originally from Cardiff, was killed on 21 August 2015 by a drone strike which was specifically approved by Philip Hammond as Secretary of State for Defence. Reporting to the House of Commons, the Prime Minister David Cameron said:

> Both Junaid Hussain and Reyaad Khan were British nationals based in Syria who were involved in actively recruiting ISIL sympathisers and seeking to orchestrate specific and barbaric attacks against the west including directing a number of planned terrorist attacks right here in Britain, such as plots to attack high profile public commemorations,

including those taking place that summer. We should be under no illusion, their intention was the murder of British citizens, so on this occasion we ourselves took action. In an act of self-defence, and after meticulous planning, Reyaad Khan was killed in a precision airstrike by an RAF remotely operated aircraft while he was travelling in a vehicle in the area of Raqqa in Syria.

Mohammed Emwazi, known as 'Jihadi John', was the executioner who cut the throat of the British aid worker Alan Hemming in August 2014. He was born in Kuwait; his family moved to Britain when he was six; in London he attended the Quintin Kynaston Community Academy in Maida Vale and then went to the University of Westminster, gaining a degree in IT. At twenty-one he returned to work in Kuwait and joined ISIS. He became the official executioner of Western prisoners, and he killed at least seven by cutting their throats. Emwazi was killed in Raqqa with British approval by a US drone on 12 November 2015, aged twenty-seven.

Sally Jones, a British jihadi, known as the 'White Widow', had played in a punk rock band in Britain, then went out to Iraq with her son in 2013. She became a leading recruiter and propagandist for ISIS and married another recruiter from Birmingham who was killed by a drone in 2015. The United Nations declared her one of the most wanted terrorists in the world. It is believed that she and her son were killed by a CIA Predator drone strike in Raqqa on 25 July 2017.

Naweed Hussain, a thirty-two-year-old man from Coventry, left his wife and children to go and fight for the Islamic State in 2015. He had been identified by British security forces in Raqqa, where he was using social media to groom jihadi brides from Britain as well as planning attacks in the UK. He was killed by a British drone in spring 2017.

Hoped-for international political assassinations 1944–73

A plan to assassinate Hitler was prepared in 1944 by the SOE, the Special Operations Executive, which had been created as a 'new instrument of war' in May 1940 to engage in clandestine activities in Europe. Their plan, known as 'Foxley', was based on their knowledge that Hitler was most vulnerable at his mountain retreat in Berchtesgaden when he took a short walk alone down to the Tea House. A sniper dressed in German combat clothes and carrying a German rifle would be parachuted into the retreat and wait to shoot Hitler as he walked down. This plan had the flavour of John Buchan about it and was abandoned in 1945. It had been strongly opposed by the head of German affairs in the SOE on the grounds that as Hitler was such an appalling military strategist he was better off alive than dead.

MI5 and MI6, the two agencies of national security, have not engaged in assassinations, although in the post-colonial period several British prime ministers expressed the hope that a particularly difficult leader of another country could be removed. At the time of the Suez Crisis in 1956 Prime Minister Anthony Eden telephoned Anthony Nutting, his Minister of State for Foreign Affairs: 'What's all this nonsense about isolating Nasser . . . I want him destroyed, can't you understand? I want him murdered, and if you and the Foreign Office don't agree then you had better come to Cabinet and explain why.' The SIS (Secret Intelligence Service) was only too glad to draw up plans to assassinate the Egyptian President Gamal Abdel Nasser, including using a poisoned dart, poisoning his favourite chocolates, and making his electric razor explode. Not surprisingly, nothing came of these.

In 1962 The Times diary reported that 'Macmillan and Kennedy apparently agreed to "liquidate" President Sukarno of Indonesia depending upon the situation and available opportunities.' The CIA considered a plan involving an air hostess who would appeal to the President's voracious sexual appetite, but nothing happened. However they must have intended to use poison or a nerve agent, since they created a euphemism: assassinating was now 'biologically immobilising'. In 1973 Maurice Oldfield became the Head of SIS and had to deal with Harold Wilson's view that it would be better if Idi Amin, the Ugandan dictator, was killed. Oldfield sent a minute to his staff telling them that SIS did not 'do' assassinations. Martin Pearce in his book *Spymaster* said that Oldfield told James Callaghan's Foreign Secretary, David Owen: 'We prefer more cerebral solutions these days, Foreign Secretary.'

II

ISRAEL

*'If someone comes to kill you,
rise up and kill him first.'*

BABYLONIAN TALMUD, PORTION 72, VERSE I

What became the state of Israel in 1948 had been the British Mandate of Palestine since the First World War. In 1920 the Balfour Declaration had promised a homeland for the Jews. The Palestinian Arabs objected, and a group of radical Jewish fighters called Lehi, which the press in Britain called the Stern Gang, founded in 1940, launched assassination attacks on British troops to force them to leave Palestine.

In 1946 MI5 told Prime Minister Attlee that there were plots by Zionists for Israel to establish five terrorist cells in Britain to assassinate Ernest Bevin, the Foreign Minister, hated because he opposed the creation of a separate Jewish state and wanted European Jews to be prevented from emigrating to Israel. The plans came to nothing, though in 1947 letter bombs were sent to several British politicians, including Bevin.

When in May 1948 David Ben-Gurion declared the establishment of the new state of Israel and defined its boundaries, it was immediately attacked by the armies of seven countries. From its very beginning Israel has lived in a state of siege, for most Arab countries want to obliterate it.

Ben-Gurion realised that Israel could not rely for its protection just on an army, a navy and an air force: it needed a top quality military and civilian intelligence service to identify plots and threats so they could be stopped before they were launched. In 1949 he therefore established an organization for military and intelligence security, which came to be called Mossad, effectively the official agency for assassinations. It was directly responsible to the prime minster, and its identity was hidden from the Israeli public. All Israeli prime ministers have looked upon Mossad as a necessary instrument of self-defence, for Jews knew from their history that in the last resort it was up to them to defend themselves. As the Israeli journalist Ronen Bergman observed, 'A people living with a sense of perpetual danger and annihilation is going to take any and all measures however extreme to obtain security, and will relate to international laws and norms in a marginal manner, if at all.'

One of Mossad's first missions was to hunt down Nazis who had been involved in the Holocaust and to kill them in whatever country they had fled to. Their big success was to track down Adolf Eichmann in 1960 and bring him back for trial in Israel. By then Mossad had over a thousand employees and started to work closely with America's CIA.

Mossad has been one of the most successful intelligence operations in the world right up to today. Ronen Bergman, an outstanding journalist, author, and recipient of international awards including a PhD from Cambridge University, gave a detailed history of its development in *Rise and Kill First* (2018). When he embarked on this book in 2010 the Israeli defence establishment and the government tried to hinder, disrupt and prevent his research. The top secret qualification that surrounds the activities of Mossad and the national security services means that very few written records are available to the public, so Bergman garnered his information from thousands of interviews with people who had worked with Mossad and the security services who wanted to tell their story.

What emerged is that the targeted assassination of specific people was at the very heart of Mossad. Bergman says: 'Since the Second World War Israel has assassinated more people than any other country in the Western world.'

> The numbers speak for themselves. Up until the start of the Second Palestinian Intifada, in September 2000, when Israel first began to respond to suicide bombings with the daily use of armed drones to perform assassinations, the state had conducted some 500 targeted killing operations. In these, at least 1,000 people were killed, both civilians and combatants. During the Second Intifada, Israel carried

out some 1,000 more operations, of which 168 succeeded. Since then, up until the writing of this book, Israel has executed some 800 targeted killing operations, almost all of which were part of the rounds of warfare against Hamas in the Gaza Strip in 2008, 2012, and 2014 or Mossad operations across the Middle East against Palestinian, Syrian, and Iranian targets. By contrast, during the presidency of George W. Bush, the United States of America carried out 48 targeted killing operations, according to one estimate, and under President Barack Obama there were 353 such attacks.

The Israeli Prime Minister has to approve that a certain person should be targeted and killed. Sometimes that decision was discussed by the cabinet. On several occasions after Yasser Arafat had emerged and was recognised internationally as the popular leader of the Palestine Liberation Organization Israeli prime ministers considered proposals for his assassination. Golda Meier, Prime Minister 1969–74, refused to sanction it, on the grounds that Israel would inevitably be blamed and that would lead not only to international condemnation but also to reprisals against Israeli ministers. On another occasion Sharon pressed strongly for Arafat's assassination, but the Cabinet was split 50/50 and he was saved. In 1997 his name was removed from the Israeli hitlist.

Israel continues to use targeted killings when its security is threatened. In May 2019, after a heavy exchange of missiles initiated by Hamas which killed four Israeli citizens though more were killed in Gaza by Israel's retaliation, Israel killed a thirty-four-year-old Hamas banker, Hamed Ahmed al-Khoudarg, responsible for arranging money from Iran, by directing a missile at his car.

From the long list of targeted killings, I have selected seven cases which show how professional Mossad has been and how it is still actively operating today:

* Tom Wilkin, 1944
* Count Folke Bernadotte, 1948
* Herberts Cukurs, 1965

* The attack during the Munich Olympics, 1972
* Khalil al-Wazir, known as Abu Jihad, 1988
* Saddam Hussein, 1992
* Fadi al-Batsh, 2018

Tom Wilkin
29 September 1944

Tom Wilkin had worked in Palestine for thirteen years and was the commander of the Jewish Unit in the CID of the British Mandate of Palestine. Using his fluent Hebrew he infiltrated some of the Jewish underground groups, including the Stern Gang, which launched assassination attacks on British troops to force them to leave Palestine. The head of the Stern Gang had been shot in February

The central figure in this 'Wanted' poster of the Palestinian Police Force is Yitzhak Shamir. This may be the only image of a terrorist and assassin who was later to become a prime minister

1942 and Yitzhak Shamir, the Gang's operations chief, decreed that Wilkin should be killed. Shamir was later to become Prime Minister of Israel.

On the morning of 29 September Wilkin left his lodgings in the Romanian Church annexe to walk to the Russian Compound to interrogate underground suspects. When he passed a grocery store a young man stood up and dropped his hat, giving the signal to two men, Shomron and Banai, that Wilkin was their target. They fired fourteen shots into him. Shomron said: 'He fell face first. A spurt of blood came out of his forehead like a fountain. It was not a pretty picture... I didn't feel anything, not even a twinge of guilt – we believed the more coffins that reached London the closer the day of freedom would be.'

The British mandate that had started in 1920 ended four years after this assassination. After the First World War Britain was beginning to withdraw from some of its international obligations, and it seems very unlikely that any of the attacks by the underground terrorist groups accelerated this process.

Count Folke Bernardotte
17 September 1948

Count Bernardotte was the grandson of Oscar II, King of Sweden. During the Second World War as head of the Swedish Red Cross he won the respect of many Europeans by arranging the exchange of prisoners of war, and saving 21,000 inmates from Nazi concentration camps.

In May 1948 Bernardotte was appointed United Nations Mediator in Palestine to settle the precise boundaries between the new country of Israel and the surrounding Arab states. That was his first priority, as war had broken out there. The proposals in his tentative peace plan were that 300,000 Arab refugees should be allowed to return to Israel, and that most of the Negev, and critically Jerusalem, should be given to the Arabs. This was unacceptable to many Jews. The Lehi or Stern Gang had planned the assassination in 1942 of Lord Moyne, the British resident Minister of State in Cairo, who was considered to be anti-Semitic because he had reduced the entry quotas for Holocaust survivors. The

Bernardotte proposals were totally unacceptable to Shamir, and notices were posted in the streets of cities: 'Advice to the Agent Bernardotte – clear out of our country.'

On 17 September 1948 three Stern assassins stopped Bernardotte's car on its journey from UN headquarters to Jewish Jerusalem: one of the three, Yehoshua Cohen, opened the car door and sprayed the occupants with a submachine gun, killing Bernardotte and his companion, a French colonel, instantaneously. The assassins were never caught.

Ben-Gurion was furious: he saw this as a challenge to his authority, so he outlawed the Lehi and arrested its members. One of the consequences of this assassination was that Ben-Gurion decided to take personal command of Mossad.

Hugh Trevor-Roper, the Regius Professor of History at Oxford, enjoyed debunking heroes and he struck at Bernardotte's reputation. He found out that it was Himmler's masseur, Felix Kersten, who had been responsible for saving 21,000 prisoners from the concentration camps: Bernardotte, as an official of the Red Cross, had only arranged the transport, and had initially refused to take any Jews, having told Himmler that he shared his racial views. Trevor Roper in 1995 said he was not absolutely certain about his allegations.

Herberts Cukurs
7 March 1965

Cukurs was a Latvian airman who participated in the mass murder of Jews when the Germans occupied Riga, the Latvian capital, in the early 1940s. He killed Jews for sport, shooting them down after telling them to run for their lives, and locked Jews in synagogues and set them on fire. He had fled to Brazil, where he started a tourist business, and that is where Mossad found 'the Butcher of Riga'.

Undercover agents persuaded Cukurs to go to Montevideo in Uruguay for a business deal, but when he met the three assassins in a hotel he soon realised he had been trapped. He threw one of them down to the ground and bit the hand

Herberts Cukurs

of another so hard that part of his finger came away. The third hitman, Ze'ev Amit, could not use his gun in the tangled mess of fighting, so he smashed a hammer into Cukurs' head again and again. They finished him off with two shots, then put his body in a suitcase with a note: 'In consideration of his personal responsibility for the murder of 30,000 Jews with horrible brutality, the condemned man has been executed' – signed by 'Those who will never forget'.

The Munich Olympics and after 1972–92

A group of Palestinians called the Black September (the name referred to the killing of many Palestinians by King Hussein of Jordan in September 1970) decided to hit Israel while the country was participating in the Olympics in Munich. Eight Black September members went to a camp in the Libyan desert to train for an attack on the Israeli team. On 5 September 1972 they raided the team's quarters, shot one athlete, and seized nine others as hostages.

They demanded the release of 234 Palestinian prisoners, and two helicopters to take them back to safety. This was agreed, and the helicopters were prepared. A German attempt to rescue the hostages and kill the terrorists was bungled: as the terrorists realised that their escape route had been blocked, they shot the two helicopter pilots and lobbed grenades into the helicopters where the nine Israeli hostages were handcuffed, waiting to leave. They and the terrorists were all killed. Two Israelis had been shot earlier, which brought the total to eleven. No attempt had been made to involve the expertise of Mossad in handling such a crisis. The Palestinians came to regard this attack as a great success, since their campaign had headed the news bulletins across the world for several days.

Israel had not expected such a well-organised attack on their nationals when they were overseas. The Prime Minister, Golda Meir, decided in revenge to track down and kill the Palestinians who were behind the attack. The title of this operation was 'The Wrath of God'. It was quite simply an eye for an eye.

The leading Palestinian figure, very close to Yasser Arafat, was Ali Hassan Salameh, nicknamed the 'Red Prince'. He had a playboy image of fast cars and beautiful girls. In 1973 Mossad traced him to the Norwegian town of Lillehammer, and sent a team. On 28 July he was identified, returning from the cinema with a young woman. They killed him with fourteen bullets but did not hurt his companion. Mission accomplished? No, because the man they shot was a Moroccan waiter called Ahmed Bouchiki and the woman was his pregnant wife. But Mossad did not give up. Six years later they succeeded, with a remote-controlled car bomb in Beirut. Ali Hassan Salameh was dead, but so were 4 people passing by, and 18 were injured. Another who was believed to have been involved in the Munich massacre was killed in Paris in 1992. This all demonstrates how extensive Mossad's networks were and how they would never give up until they had killed all their targets.

Khalil al-Wazir, known as Abu Jihad
16 April 1988

Abu Jihad, 'the Father of the Struggle', was a co-founder of the Fateh Party who masterminded several terrorist attacks on Israeli targets in the 1970s and 1980s. In one in 1978, on an Israeli bus near Tel-Aviv, 38 Israelis were killed and 78 injured; it became known as the 'Coastal Road Massacre'. He had become in effect Yasser Arafat's right-hand man. In the autumn of 1987 he had claimed that he was the prime mover behind the widespread demonstrations on the West Bank known as the Intifada, in which over a thousand Palestinians were killed by Israelis. In 1988 Prime Minister Rabin was persuaded at last to give the go-ahead to assassinate him.

As Abu Jihad lived in Tunisia, some 1,250 miles from Israel, a military and

Khalil Ibrahim al-Wazir, 'Abu Jihad'

naval operation involving helicopters, missile-boats and a mobile hospital was planned. Twenty-six commandos were landed about a third of a mile from Abu Jihad's lightly guarded house on a moonless night. Their leader, Nahum Lev, and another soldier dressed as a woman pretended to be a courting couple carrying what appeared to be a large box of chocolates, but which actually concealed a gun with a silencer. The Israeli commandos had to be sure that the man they had seen entering the villa just after midnight was in fact Abu Jihad: they managed to tap into a telephone call he was making that confirmed it, so the operation could go ahead. Lev first shot Abu Jihad's bodyguard, who had fallen asleep in his car, and a gardener. Then he burst into the house and found Abu Jihad in his bedroom. He later said: 'I shot him with a long burst of fire. He was a dead man walking. I shot him without hesitation.' Five other Israelis also fired into his body. Neither

Nahum Lev, the assassin

Abu Jihad's wife nor his children were shot or wounded.

The Israelis had identified Abu Jihad as a target for assassination twenty-three years earlier. This daring raid showed not only the professional efficiency of Mossad but again their determination never to give up.

Saddam Hussein
1992

After Saddam Hussein's failure to seize Kuwait, and after America had left him in power, Mossad believed that he was actively planning to create weapons of mass destruction – nuclear bombs. In fact he wasn't, but Mossad decided that there was sufficient evidence to justify his assassination, and in 1992 the outgoing Israeli Prime Minister Yitzhak Shamir and the incoming Prime Minister Yitzhak Rabin both agreed to give Mossad the go-ahead.

Getting close to Saddam Hussein in Iraq was however almost impossible, particularly as Mossad always intended for their assassins to escape. They decided that they would have to attempt to kill Hussein when he was engaged in a private family activity, where they could be assured that it was him and not one of his many doubles. They planned to attack him at his family's plot in the cemetery at Tikrit when he was attending the funeral of a relative or close friend. The funeral they chose was that of Barzan Al-Tikriti, the Iraqi Ambassador to the United Nations.

Mossad then built a replica of the Hussein family cemetery in the Negev desert to rehearse the killing. Helicopters would land some distance away and discharge jeeps which had guided missiles concealed in their roofs, and they would move close to the cemetery. In a dry run Israeli soldiers and members of Mossad represented Hussein's family party. This was to be followed by a wet run, when the real assassins would discharge live missiles at their target, now a model of Hussein. Both runs unfortunately had the same codeword, 'Send a cab'. The commander in the jeeps heard the codeword, and thinking that the dry run was over discharged the missiles: these landed in the middle of the Israeli soldiers and officials, killing five and wounding many others. After this appalling accident the plan to assassinate Saddam Hussein was dropped. He had been saved by the incompetence of Mossad.

Fadi al-Batsh
21 April 2018

Fadi al-Batsh, a thirty-five-year-old scientist, was a lecturer in power engineering at the University of Kuala Lumpur. Allegedly he was helping Hamas to manufacture rockets and improve their accuracy. On Saturday 21 April 2018 he was walking to his mosque in the residential area of Setapak when two men on a motorbike fired at least ten rounds from a handgun and four of them hit al-Batsh in his head.

Hamas immediately accused Mossad of assassinating him and called him a martyr. Palestinian websites said he was related to a senior official in the Islamic Jihad terrorist group, but his father denied that. Hamas provided a guard of honour at his mourning tent.

The Israeli Defence Minister would neither confirm nor deny that Mossad had a hand in the death, but he went on to say; 'This man was not a saint. We

Killed in Malaysia, honoured by Hamas

have no interest in shedding a tear for him.'

Western and Middle Eastern intelligence officials have been quoted as saying that al-Batsh may have been involved in negotiating arms deals with North Korea through Malaysia.

Yasser Arafat
1929-2004

By the end of the 1960s Yasser Arafat had become the acknowledged leader of the Palestinians, and Mossad decided that he should be assassinated. It was very difficult to carry that out in the West Bank or in Gaza, as Arafat frequently moved location and was heavily protected. In 1970 it was decided to use a sniper to shoot him when he was attending a meeting with Gaddafi in Libya. However the Prime Minister, Golda Meier, refused to approve the assassination: Israel would be blamed by the world, and it could promote reprisals against Israeli leaders.

After Arafat's address to the United Nations in 1974 the head of counter-terrorism in Mossad recognised that his standing in the world had changed: 'He's the head of the snake but the world has given him legitimacy and killing him would put Israel into an unnecessary political imbroglio.' Eventually his name was removed from the hit list.

In 1982 Ariel Sharon, the Israeli Defence Minister who was principally responsible for the invasion of Southern Lebanon, asserted that Arafat was 'the most dangerous enemy of Israel' and had to be killed. He believed that after Arafat was killed the Palestine Liberation Organization would break up into dissident groups, so he set up a task force codenamed 'Saltfish'. Several attempts were made, but Arafat was always one step ahead. In 1984 he was forced to leave Beirut but in one location he was recognised; Mossad managed to place a sniper who photographed Arafat, but Sharon was instructed by Begin not to have him shot.

Sharon did not give up. It was discovered at a later date in 1982 that Arafat was in Greece and would be taking a private plane to Cairo. This seemed the

This photograph was taken by a sniper of Sayeret Matkal Commando. The Prime Minister, Menachem Begin, showed it to the American mediator to prove that Israel could have killed Arafat had they wished to.

perfect opportunity. Two Israeli fighter planes were dispatched with the order to be prepared to engage with a civilian plane. After twenty-five minutes of the flight Mossad expressed some doubts as to whether Arafat was actually on board. A few moments later, just in time, they discovered that the passengers were Arafat's younger brother Fathi, accompanied by thirty wounded Palestinian children. If Mossad had brought down that plane it would have been a major disaster.

In 2004 Sharon's view had still not changed: he said that Arafat was 'a pathological liar, a murderer who organised the killing of women and children'. At a meeting in the White House President George W. Bush demanded that Sharon should promise not to kill Arafat, and finally Sharon reluctantly agreed.

Shortly afterwards Arafat died unexpectedly in France. His body was examined by French, Swiss and Russian teams and some found traces of polonium. That was disputed, but it raised the suspicion that somehow Israel and Sharon were involved in his death.

Anwar Sadat
6 October 1981

Israel was not involved in this assassination, but it did have a significant effect upon subsequent Israeli policy.

Anwar Sadat was brought up in a village in the Nile Delta, working on his father's farm, and went to a Koranic school where he learnt the 114 chapters of the Koran by heart. He joined the army and by the age of twenty became a second lieutenant. After the end of the Second World War he joined a campaign to end Britain's involvement with Egypt; he was charged with assassinating the Egyptian Minister of Finance, and although he was acquitted he later accepted responsibility for it. He supported Colonel Nasser's coup, was appointed Vice President in 1969, and on Nasser's death in 1970 became President of Egypt.

Sadat replaced Russian support for Egypt with American. In 1973 he launched the Yom Kippur War to win back control of the Sinai Peninsula, which Israel had seized in the 1967 war. Initially it went very well for Egypt, but Israel, strongly supported by America, forced him to retreat. Encouraged by Henry Kissinger, peace negotiations were started which eventually led to the Camp David Accord of 1978. Sadat went to Israel and spoke to the Knesset, calling for peace. Sadat for Egypt and Begin for Israel were awarded the Nobel Peace Prize. The rest of the Arab world reacted with great hostility, shocked that an Egyptian leader even visited Israel, and Egypt was suspended from the Arab League. In order to suppress domestic opposition, principally from the Muslim Brotherhood, Sadat became much more authoritarian, suspending parliament and banning strikes, and in September 1981 he had two thousand people arrested.

The moment of the assassination

To celebrate the day in 1973 when Egyptian soldiers had crossed the Suez Canal and won back the Sinai, he ordered a great military parade on 6 October 1981. Sadat had lived with the threat of assassination, but thought he would be quite safe in front of his army's military parade. A camouflaged truck stopped in front of the viewing stand and four men with submachine guns and AK47 rifles, led by Lieutenant Khalid El-Islambouli, jumped out, threw two grenades, and raked the stand with machine gun fire. Sadat was hit four times and died two hours later. The assassins had killed two others and wounded thirty; they just missed killing Sadat's deputy, Mubarak. This assassination was planned by the Muslim Brotherhood, which intended to establish a fundamentalist Muslim government in Egypt similar to that of Iran.

The four assassins were executed, and Mubarak became President.

This assassination did not end the secular character of the Egyptian Government, which was reinforced by Mubarak. He then became a target for assassination. When I visited him in the late 1980s at his palace outside Cairo all of us had body searches and our car had to go through a tank trap and drive through huge iron gates before I reached the President's presence. Mubarak was not assassinated, but later overthrown by the Muslim Brotherhood.

Yitzhak Rabin
4 November 1995

'I don't believe a Jew will kill a Jew.'

Before he entered politics by winning a Labour seat in the Knesset in 1973, Yitzhak Rabin had spent much of his earlier life in the army fighting Palestinians and the countries that supported them – Egypt, Syria and Jordan. He was Chief of the General Staff during the victorious Six Day War in 1967 when Israel made massive territorial gains, capturing the West Bank, the Gaza Strip, the Golan Heights and the Sinai Peninsula. Rabin became a national hero. He was Prime Minister from 1974 to 1977.

In 1992 Rabin was elected Chairman of the Labour Party, beating Shimon Peres to the post, and became Prime Minister again, promising to forward the Israel-Palestine peace process. He was a strong supporter of the Oslo Accords brokered by President Bill Clinton and sealed by a handshake with Yasser Arafat on the White House lawn in September 1993 – the picture was flashed around the world. The Accords created the Palestinian National Authority, and Israel ceded partial control of the Gaza Strip and parts of the West Bank. Arafat renounced violence and officially recognised Israel, which was unacceptable to many Palestinians and neighbouring Arab countries. Rabin replied by recognising the Palestine Liberation Organization. These were truly significant moves which were recognised with a grant of the Nobel Peace Prize shared by Rabin, Peres and Arafat.

Rabin accelerated the process with a peace treaty with Jordan, and in October 1994 agreed to the withdrawal of Israeli troops from the Palestinian cities and villages on the West Bank. The responsibility of government was transferred to over a million Arabs. Rabin was attacked on both flanks – on one by the terrorist group Hamas, determined to destroy the state of Israel, and on the other by the

Yitzhak Rabin, Bill Clinton and Yasser Arafat

Likud Party and many Israelis who looked upon the surrender of territory with horror. He knew he was risking his life in pushing ahead so strongly, but he felt assured of his safety: 'I don't believe a Jew will kill a Jew.' However those on the Right held meetings condemning him; his photograph was burnt; and he was depicted in Nazi uniform.

On 4 November 1995 a huge peace rally to support him was held in Tel Aviv; 50,000 people were expected, but five times that number cheered and chanted, 'Rabin, Rabin, Rabin'. He began his speech: 'I want to thank each of you for standing up against violence, for peace.' Both he and Peres were persuaded not to plunge into this great crowd, and made their way to the official car park. That was meant to be a secure area, but it was full of people who should not have been there, including a twenty-five-year-old Israeli law student, Yigal Amir. He stepped forward and fired three shots, hitting Rabin in his chest, abdomen and back. As he had used dumdum bullets there was no chance of survival.

In his trial Amir proudly admitted to the shooting, justifying it: 'I acted alone on God's orders . . . I did it to save the state. He who endangers the Jewish people his end is death. He deserved to die and I did the job for the Jewish people.' At his trial he was arrogant, proudly asserting the words of the extreme Right wing. He was sentenced to life imprisonment: only Nazi war criminals could be executed. Leaders from across the world attended Rabin's funeral. Arafat wanted to do as well, but was persuaded not to as it would have provoked Right-wing protests; however, wearing civilian clothes and dark glasses he went privately to console Mrs Rabin: 'We have lost a great man.' He also knew that things would only get worse.

This assassination robbed Israel of a man who was able to make peace with the Palestinians, and the peace process lost its momentum. The next election was won by Benjamin Netanyahu, who had opposed the Oslo Accords, shouting at Rabin in the Knesset: 'the Bible is our deed to the land'. It would not be shared with any other state. To confirm that, he increased the building of settlements on the West Bank, known to Israelis as Judea and Samaria, and they were to remain firmly under Israeli control. There are now 600,000 Israelis living among 2.7 million Palestinians.

Rabin's assassination became a watershed in Israel's move to the Right. If he had survived he would not have extended Jewish settlements on the West Bank, and things might have been very different. His assassination was the prelude to the end of the Two State solution.

The suicide bomber

It took some time for the Palestinians in the West Bank and Hamas in Gaza to devise a counter-measure that was to inflict considerable damage on the population of Israel: that was the suicide bomber.

Hamas had a brilliant bomb designer, Ayyash, known as 'The Engineer'. He had developed the most effective bombs so successfully that Peres, as Prime Minister, signed the red page approving his assassination, which was carried out in January 1996. In the month before he was killed, Ayyash had trained a group of Hamas activists to make small lethal devices which could be put into the pockets of jackets that would be worn like waistcoats. The suicide vest was born.

On the day of his death Hamas operatives started to recruit suicide bombers. One of them said: 'The gates of Hell have been opened.'

One of the first attacks was made on a bus in Jerusalem, killing 26 people. That was followed by an attack on a military post, killing one soldier and wounding 36 others. Israel did not know how to stop this campaign, and that was one of the reasons that led to Netanyahu becoming Prime Minister after Rabin's assassination. In 2001 a campaign of suicide bombing took off with weekly attacks, killing in that year 124 men, women and children, and wounding 683; in 2002 120 were killed, and in 2003 135.

The Palestinian Liberation Front did not officially engage in assassinations, but there were groups of Palestinians that did. One was led by Maher al-Taher, who lived in exile in Damascus but led the proscribed Popular Front for the Liberation of Palestine (PFLP). The world learnt more about the PFLP after the visit of Jeremy Corbyn to Tunis in September 2014 to attend a memorial service for Palestinian leaders who had been killed there in 1985. He was photographed holding a wreath at a side event, near the memorials to the Palestinian terrorists

Maher al-Taher and Jeremy Corbyn in Tunis in 2014

who had killed eleven Israeli athletes at the Munich Olympic Games. Not long afterwards, the PFLP launched a savage attack in Jerusalem on 18 November 2014: two men wielding axes, knives and a gun burst into an ultra-Orthodox synagogue and killed four rabbis and a policeman. The assassins were shot dead. The PLFP claimed responsibility for what they did and called it 'heroic'. Recently a photograph emerged of Corbyn standing next to Maher al-Taher at the 2014 event, adding to the embarrassment of the Labour Leader who had been struggling for months to show that the Labour Party he led was not anti-Semitic.

One group of Palestinian terrorists that particularly concerned Mossad was known as the Al-Aqsa Martyrs Brigade. It was established in 2000 by Arafat's Fatah Party to exert pressure on Israel to withdraw from the territories it had seized in the 1967 war. Attacks by its members on military (not civilian) targets in 2001 and 2002 led to the second Intifada. Mossad's reaction was to take out some of the leaders on the West Bank, but this backfired. The old leaders were more experienced and cautious; lower-level terrorists were less experienced and tended to respond by becoming even more militant. This led Mossad to stop targeting the older leaders.

III

RUSSIA

'When there is no person, there is no problem.'
STALIN

Russian history can be described as periods of despotic rule tempered by assassination. Five of the twenty Romanov tsars were assassinated: Peter III (1762), Ivan VI (1764), Paul I (1801), Alexander II (1881) and Nicholas II (1917). A sixth, Alexander III, narrowly escaped assassination in 1887, on the fifth anniversary of the assassination of his father – which had been planned by Lenin's older brother. From 1917 the Bolshevik regime used assassination as a political instrument to eliminate opponents, dissidents, critics and rivals, both within Russia and in other countries – a practice carried on by Stalin and Putin.

Peter III
17 July 1762

On 28 June 1762 Catherine, with the help of her lover, Orlov, rallied the army at St Petersburg, arrested her husband, Peter III, and forced him to abdicate in her favour as Catherine II. She named her son Paul as her heir and became one of the most successful and famous rulers of Russia for the next thirty-four years. Soon afterwards Peter was strangled, but it was not known whether Catherine had a hand in it. A disastrous marriage from the first, it had lasted for seventeen years. He took mistresses and she took lovers. Catherine described her husband as 'an idiot', 'a drunkard from Holstein' and 'a good for nothing'.

Her coup was launched when she heard that her husband was about to arrest one of her co-conspirators. The key to her success was that she went at once to the Ismailovsky Regiment seeking their support, and the army then took her to the Semenovsky Barracks where the clergy were waiting to ordain

Peter III and Catherine II

her as sole ruler of Russia.

Catherine the Great also decided to assassinate Ivan VI, who had been tsar briefly as a child before being deposed, since he also had a claim to the throne.

Paul I
23 March 1801

Catherine the Great had little time for her son Paul. He was not at all involved in her government; she married him off to a German princess, and exiled him to an estate far from St Petersburg. But he succeeded on his mother's death in 1796. Some were doubtful about his sanity. He alienated several powerful families, who decided that he should be deposed and replaced by his own son, Grand Duke Alexander. After a dinner party attended by Alexander the conspirators, led by General Leo Bennigsen, a Hanoverian in the Russian service, and Count von Pahlen, the military commander of St Petersburg, entered the palace, forced their way into Paul's room, and strangled him. It is not known whether Alexander knew what was going to happen, but when he became tsar he did not punish the assassins: the court doctor was told to record the death of his father as due to apoplexy.

Alexander II
31 March 1881

Alexander II was the first tsar to recognise that reforms were necessary to make Russia's system of government more efficient and more liberal. He introduced extensive changes: a new penal code, with trial in open court; judges appointed for life; a jury system; military conscription, previously just for serfs, extended to all social classes; and flogging abolished. Local self-government was introduced for rural districts with some degree of local taxation, and university education was promoted. His most significant reform was the abolition of serfdom in 1861, for which he was known as 'Alexander the Liberator'.

'Am I a wild beast they would hound to death?'

When he succeeded in 1855 there were 50 million serfs in a total population of 60 million. They lived for the most part as farm labourers, obliged to work for their owners and debarred from owning land. They required the consent of their owner to be married, and they could be ordered to serve for twenty-five years in Siberia, which was close to a sentence of death. By abolishing serfdom Alexander alienated the nobility and the other owners of serfs.

Four attempts were made to assassinate him – all in St Petersburg, apart from the second. The first was in 1866; the second in 1867 at the Exposition Universelle in Paris, when the pistol of the would-be assassin, a student acting alone, misfired; and the third in 1879 – a student again, who fired five shots that missed. The fourth was on 17 February 1880, when a Russian terrorist group called the People's Will planted a bomb in the main dining room of the Winter Palace in St Petersburg: it killed 11 people and wounded 30, but the royal family escaped,

Sophia Perovskaya

having arrived late. The People's Will was the best organised of several revolutionary groups in Moscow. It was led by Sophia Perovskaya, daughter of the Governor General of St Petersburg; trained as a teacher, she came to embrace very radical ideas, and had been involved in the Winter Palace bombing.

On 17 March 1881 Alexander signed a decree to establish a parliamentary assembly, the Duma, which was to be elected. This was the first time that any tsar had been prepared to share his absolute power. On 31 March Alexander did what he always did on a Sunday, which was to travel in the bomb-proof carriage given to him by Napoleon III – who had been lucky enough to survive a bomb attack – to the cathedral, along a familiar route. Sophia Perovskaya had planted four assassins along the Tsar's route; one of the younger ones, Nikolai Rysakov, was to throw the first bomb. On this occasion the Tsar was accompanied by two sleighs carrying the Chief of

Police, Dvorzhitsky, and the Chief of the Royal Guards. The first bomb landed under his carriage, killing one Cossack. Alexander stepped down to find out what had happened, and before any guard could stand in his way he was hit by another bomb, thrown at his feet by a second student, who shouted, 'It is too early to thank God.' The Chief of Police recorded what happened next:

> I was deafened by the new explosion, burned, wounded and thrown to the ground. Suddenly, amid the smoke and snowy fog, I heard His Majesty's weak voice cry, 'Help!' Gathering what strength I had, I jumped up and rushed to the Tsar. His Majesty was half-lying, half-sitting, leaning on his right arm. Thinking he was merely wounded heavily, I tried to lift him but the Tsar's legs were shattered, and the blood poured out of them. Twenty people, with wounds of varying degree, lay on the sidewalk and on the street. Some managed to stand, others to crawl, still others tried to get out from beneath bodies that had fallen on them. Through the snow, debris, and blood you could see fragments of clothing, epaulets, sabers, and bloody chunks of human flesh.

The second student had been killed by his bomb. A third student was discovered waiting with a bomb in case the others had failed. Alexander was taken to the Winter Palace, bleeding to death, with his legs torn away, his stomach open, and his face mutilated.

Within days Sophia and other members of the People's Will were arrested and hanged. The first woman terrorist to be executed in Russia, she told her mother not to grieve: 'I have lived by my convictions and it would not have been possible to have acted otherwise.'

These attacks on Alexander's life were among the first to use dynamite (invented by the Swedish chemist Alfred Nobel) in its more malleable and destructive form, gelignite. The chief bomb-maker of the People's Will was Nikolai Kibalchich – honoured by the Soviet Union by naming a crater on the dark side of the moon after him.

A contemporary Russian carte de visite depicting the assassination.

This murder led to a major suppression of civil liberties. Alexander's proposals to create a form of elected government were abandoned, and a move to a constitutional monarchy was stopped. Had it been allowed to go ahead and bed down, it is possible that the Bolshevik Revolution of 1917 would never have occurred. This was an assassination that achieved the very opposite of what the assassins wanted.

Following the assassination of Alexander II, one of the most powerful secret services, OKHRANA, was established by the tsarist regime. By the end of the nineteenth century it had created a network of more than 20,000 informers. Its principal purpose was to disrupt the operation of the People's Will and other terrorist groups. The revolutionary groups in Russia embraced assassination as a major weapon to win public support: it 'would awaken even the sleepiest philistines and force them against their will to think political'. The Combat Organisation in 1902 assassinated the Interior Minister at point-blank range and organised the assassination of Grand Duke Sergei in 1905.

Grand Duke Sergei Alexandrovich
15 February 1905
Grand Duchess Elizabeth Feodorovna
17 July 1918

Grand Duke Sergei, Tsar Nicholas II's uncle, held the post of Governor General of Moscow. He was one of the most reactionary members of the Romanov dynasty, expelling 20,000 Jews from Moscow and severely suppressing a students' revolt. He even forbade his wife Elizabeth to read Tolstoy's *Anna Karenina*, as it might raise 'unhealthy curiosity and molest emotions'.

An attempt to assassinate Sergei at the Bolshoi Theatre in Moscow on 15 February 1905 was abandoned, since he was accompanied by his wife and their two adopted children. Two days later, however, as he travelled alone in a carriage to his office, a bomb was thrown and landed in his lap. He was blown to pieces and his wife later arrived to pick up some of them. The assassin was a Social revolutionary and poet named Ivan Kaliayev, who described what he did: 'I threw the bomb from less than four steps. I was taken by the explosions. I saw the carriage flew to pieces . . . My overcoat was strewn with splinters of wood all around, it was torn and burnt, there was blood on my face . . .'

The Grand Duchess Elizabeth forgave Kaliayev and was prepared to plead for his life with the Tsar if he repented, but he did not: 'I killed Sergei Alexandrovich because he was a weapon of tyranny. I was taking revenge for the people.' He told the judge who sentenced him: 'Learn to look at the advancing revolution right in the face.'

After the death of her husband, Grand Duchess Elizabeth built the Convent of Mary and Martha which was devoted to looking after the poor of Moscow. The Revolutionary Government in 1917 asked her to move into the Kremlin, but she stayed in the convent. Kaiser Wilhelm, who had once been in love with her, tried to bring her out safely, but his ambassador to Russia was assassinated. She and other members of the ruling dynasty, including Grand Duke Sergei Mikhailovich, three sons of Grand Duke Constantine, the son of Grand Duke

Elizabeth, the Romanov Saint

Paul, and Prince Vladimir Paley, were rounded up and taken to the Urals. On 18 July, the day after Nicholas II and his family had been assassinated, they were thrown down an abandoned mineshaft with heavy lumber and hand grenades lobbed after them. After the murder squad had left, a peasant heard hymns being sung from the pit. When the White Russians later captured the area they removed the bodies, and found that the head of one boy was bandaged with a handkerchief belonging to Elizabeth.

In 1981 Elizabeth was canonised by the Russian Orthodox Church – the only victim of assassination so honoured.

Grigori Rasputin
30 December 1916

'If I die the Emperor will soon lose his crown.'

Little is known of Rasputin's early life apart from the fact that he married at twenty-two and had three children. In 1897, in his late twenties, he went to a monastery where he learned to read and write, and became a self-made holy man who developed his own doctrine for salvation that owed much to his own voracious sexual appetite. His followers had first to commit a sin, usually of a sexual nature, and then he would redeem them. He acquired devoted followers, won over by his passionate oratory and hypnotic eyes; they called him 'Father Grigor, our saviour' and offered up their wives and daughters to be saved. Rasputin became immediately recognisable as the unwashed holy man, with straggly hair, dishevelled clothes, and blackened fingernails.

Rasputin had a reputation as a faith healer and in 1906 he was introduced to Tsarina Alexandra, who was preoccupied with the haemophilia of her son, Alexei, the heir to the throne. After the laying-on of hands, prayers and possibly hypnosis, some of Alexei's pain was reduced sufficiently for Alexandra to believe that Rasputin had some miraculous powers. He won the confidence of the Tsar and Tsarina so successfully that they turned to him for advice on many other matters.

The Russian nobility hated the powerful position Rasputin had carved out for himself and several assassinations were planned but not implemented. In November 1916, speaking in the Duma, Vladimir Purishkevich called for his death. He and Prince Felix Yusupov decided to assassinate Rasputin at the Prince's palace on 29 December. Rasputin was hoping to meet the Prince's beautiful wife, so he put on his best clothes – a light blue embroidered silk shirt, velvet trousers, and polished black boots. Arriving after midnight, he ate several cakes containing cyanide and drank three spiked glasses of his beloved Madeira, but that had no effect. He continued to sing and dance, calling for more music. Yusupov was the first to shoot him, in the chest, but Rasputin, foaming

Prince Felix Yusupov, one of the assassins and his wife.

Rasputin dead at last

at the mouth, grasped the Prince by the throat and then chased him on all fours. Purishkevich then shot him in the face. They wrapped his body in heavy linen and threw it into the River Neva, where it was discovered two days later under the ice. An examination showed that he had water in his lungs, which meant that he must still have been alive when he was thrown into the river.

Rasputin's death was received with universal rejoicing, and no-one except the Tsarina wanted to punish the assassins: they were heroes. He was an irritant in the political tragedy that was engulfing Russia. If the Russian nobility had had any sense or talent, they could have assumed control of the ramshackle government machine before the popular revolution did. But instead they assassinated the mystical mad monk whose power and influence they had exaggerated, believing quite absurdly that his removal would save the Romanovs – but no one could save that dynasty from what would soon happen.

Nicholas II and his family
17 July 1918

Following the February Revolution in 1917 Nicholas II and his family were arrested, and in October they were all moved to Ipatev House in Ekaterinburg, a large city in the Urals.

On 17 July 1918 Nicholas was woken by Yakov Yurovski, the last commandant at Ipatev House, and told that he and his family should go down to the cellar because there were disturbances in the city that threatened their safety. So Nicholas, his wife Alexandra, their son Alexei, and their four daughters, Olga, Tatyana, Maria and Anastasia, all went down. Nicolas was carrying his son in his arms. It was a small room; Nicholas and Alexandra were asked to sit in two chairs and the children to

Nicholas and his family

stand around them. Yurovski then told them that the Urals Regional Executive Committee had decided that they should be executed, and before Nicholas could say anything he was shot in the chest and the guards fired their pistols to kill the rest. Yurovski found the little boy, Alexei, still groaning and so he shot him three times. Some of the daughters were also bayoneted by the guards.

While these murders were happening lorries outside were revved up to try and cover the noise of the shooting. The bodies were then taken in a truck to a disused mine and dumped in a heap with all their clothes which acted as tinder, covered in petrol, and set alight. Their remains were then thrown down a mineshaft.

Lenin in Moscow was given the news at 9pm on 17 July. A committee attended

Yakov Yurovski – the executioner

by him and Trotsky put out a statement that the Tsar had been shot, but his family had been moved to a place of safety. After the murders Lenin was very deft in erasing all traces of responsibility for the execution of the Romanovs.

Who actually approved the assassination? Lenin was planning for Nicholas to be tried in Moscow, a proposal keenly supported by Trotsky, but during the summer of 1918 Lenin had chided the Bolsheviks for lacking the necessary mercilessness towards the enemies of the state, thus endorsing an environment of violence. Filipp Goloshchëkin, the military commissar of the Urals Regional Soviet Executive Committee, visited Lenin on 12 July; what they talked about has not been revealed, but it is clear that Lenin did not forbid him to kill Nicholas. On 14 July Goloshchëkin and his deputy Anuchin were joined by Safarov, one of the most militant members of the Executive Committee, whose editorial after the event read: 'He lived too long, enjoying the indulgence of the revolution like a crowned murderer.' All three went for a walk in the woods, a practice favoured by Bolsheviks when they wanted complete secrecy, for there would be no prying eyes or listening ears. They decided the fate of the

The Ipatev House cellar

Romanovs. It was left to Yurovski to recruit a firing squad.

The Bolshevik leaders were faced with a real crisis since the Czechoslovak Legion, a Russian troop including Czech and Slovak prisoners of war, were about to re-enter the Great War on the Allied side, and they were advancing on Ekaterinburg. Trotsky was concerned about their number and wanted them to be disarmed, but they held together and recruited supporters who wanted to overthrow the Bolsheviks. Joined by the White Army of imperialist Russians, they quickly took control of the railway stations on the Trans-Siberian Railway; the next big station was Ekaterinburg.

That sealed the fate of the imperial family, because they could not be allowed to fall into the hands of the White Army. On 25 July, eight days after the assassination, the Czechoslovak Legion marched into Ekaterinburg unopposed.

The burial site was discovered by chance in 1979 but not revealed until 1989. President Boris Yeltsin ordered that on 17 July 1998, eighty years to the day after they had been murdered, the imperial family's remains should be re-interred in the Cathedral of Peter and Paul in St Petersburg.

THE BOLSHEVIK REGIME

Vladimir Lenin
3 August 1918

In 1918 Lenin, the inspirational leader of the Bolshevik Revolution, was almost killed by two people in a group of Socialist revolutionaries that he had been addressing at a factory. As he was leaving the meeting, he was approached by two women who wanted to question him, Fanny and Dora Kaplan. Fanny then fired two shots at point-blank range at his neck and shoulder. She had a record of violence, having been imprisoned for attempting to kill a Tsarist official, and had only recently been released from a Siberian prison. The Bolsheviks considered that she was demented and she was shot without a trial.

Lenin was well enough to tell his driver to take him to his home rather than to a hospital, for there he feared that Tsarist sympathisers or other Socialist revolutionaries would make another attempt to kill him. The doctors who treated his wounds found that his lung had been damaged, but they decided not to remove the two bullets.

From that moment his health became a major concern, and it certainly contributed to his early death aged fifty-four in 1924. In 1921 he was seriously ill, with prolonged headaches and insomnia; in 1922 he had a stroke which left him partially paralysed; in 1923 a more severe stroke robbed him of his ability to speak; in 1924 he fell into a coma and died.

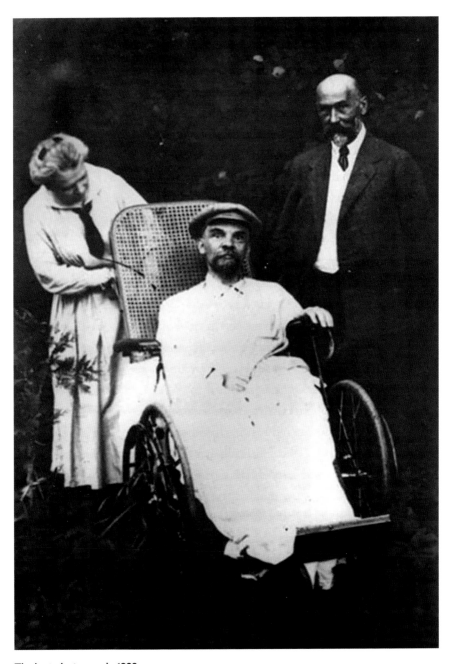

The last photograph, 1923

THE STALIN REGIME

Stalin, having assumed absolute power in 1928 after expelling Trotsky, had no qualms about using assassination as a political weapon. In the Great Terror of 1934–8 he used Russian courts as instruments of judicial assassination that drenched Russia in blood: 1.6 million dissidents, defectors, Party officials, military officers and intelligence agents were arrested and tortured, and 681,692 were shot.

Sergei Kirov
1 December 1934

'Russia drenched in blood'

Kirov was one of the old Bolsheviks who started his career in the revolutionary outbreak of 1905 and was first imprisoned in 1906. By 1934 he was second to Stalin, but his views were beginning to diverge and he wanted a more moderate approach to the government of Russia. In January that year, in the seventeenth Party Congress which celebrated the success of the first Five Year Plan, the delegates were asked on the last day to delete the names of those they were voting against: Kirov attracted only three negative votes, whereas Stalin had over one hundred, and according to some as many as three hundred. As Kirov looked upon Stalin as a friend, he discussed this result with him.

Stalin saw that he was surrounded by enemies, and over the next three years he would have more than half of the two thousand delegates to the Congress arrested and a third executed. He was not prepared to tolerate anyone who was more popular, and this meant that Kirov was doomed. Robert Conquest's book, *Stalin and the Kirov Murder*, gives a detailed account of what Stalin did. He charged Genrikh Yagoda, the head of the NKVD (officially the law enforcement agency), to assassinate Kirov; Yagoda passed the order on to his aide Vania Zaporozhets; and Zaporozhets selected as the assassin Leonid Nikolayev. The latter tried twice and was arrested for having a gun near the presence of Kirov,

Two old friends – Kirov and Stalin

Zinoviev, Kamenev and Bukharin – three old friends assassinated by Stalin

but the NKVD released him. On 1 December 1934 he managed to penetrate Kirov's well-guarded headquarters in Leningrad and killed him with a shot to the head.

On the following day Stalin personally interviewed Nikolayev and asked him why he had shot Kirov. Nikolayev pointed to the NKVD, saying, 'Ask them.' On the same day Kirov's old personal bodyguard, Borisov, who had been a key witness to the killing, was himself killed in a car accident while in the custody of the NKVD. Yagoda and all the NKVD officers involved in Kirov's death were shot. Three venerable Bolshevik leaders – Zinoviev, Kamenev and Bukharin – were arrested and imprisoned in 1934 and 1936 put on a show trial where they were forced to admit complicity in Kirov's assassination and told by Stalin that if they pleaded guilty they would not be executed. They pleaded guilty, and the day after the verdict they were shot.

Leon Trotsky
20 August 1940

'Stalin seeks my death.'

It was Trotsky who had planned the detailed operation of the Revolution, with the Bolshevik occupation of key government buildings on the night of 23–24 October 1917, and it was Trotsky's partnership with Lenin that ensured its success. As Foreign Minister Trotsky negotiated peace with Germany. He became the Commissar for War, and converted a ragbag of small units into a disciplined military machine controlled from the centre of the Party: the Red Army. He used conscription to increase that from 300,000 to 1,000,000, and then to 3,000,000. It was this that defeated the White Army.

Following Lenin's death in 1924 there was a struggle for power between Stalin and Trotsky, which Stalin eventually won through his mastery of political intrigue and a cold determination to become the supreme ruler. In 1925 Trotsky was removed as Commissar for War, in 1927 expelled from the Party, and by 1928 he had been exiled to Alma Ata on the border with Mongolia. In 1929 he was expelled from the Soviet Union altogether. He then sought to live in Turkey, in France and in Norway, but was expelled from each of these in turn, and finally settled in Mexico in 1937. There he deluged the world with articles, pamphlets and books, the most famous being *The Revolution Betrayed*, attacking Stalin for executing all the remaining Trotskyites. Stalin wanted these attacks to stop, and he started his revenge by killing Trotsky's son after kidnapping him from a Paris hospital in 1938. In June 1940 Trotsky wrote in an article: 'Stalin seeks my death.'

On 23 May 1940 a team of twenty military and police officers, led by the Stalinist Mexican artist David Alfaro, hurled bombs at Trotsky's villa and raked it with machine gun fire. Trotsky and his wife only escaped by hiding under their bed. Stalin's secret police then fed into his circle an agent, Ramón Mercader, who lived under the alias of Frank Jackson: he had seduced an American Trotskyist, Sylvia Ageloff, and she provided access to Trotsky's villa. (He spent some of his spare time learning how to use an ice axe by climbing volcanoes near Mexico

City.) He offered to write articles for Trotsky, and asked to show him one he had specially prepared on 20 August 1940. They went together into Trotsky's study;

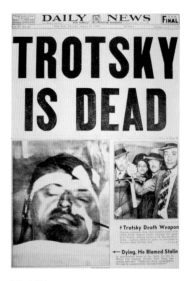

when Trotsky sat down at his desk Mercader slipped the ice axe out of his raincoat pocket and crashed it into Trotsky's skull. Later he said: 'The man screamed in such a way I will never forget as long as I live.' Trotsky managed to stop a second blow and get out of his office to call for help. The guards asked him whether they should kill Mercader, but Trotsky replied, 'Impermissible to kill, he must be forced to talk.' Trotsky died in hospital 26 hours later.

When Mercader was released from his Mexican prison in 1960 he was personally welcomed by Nikita Khrushchev and made a Hero of the Soviet Union. Liquidation of enemies of the people abroad remained part of the KGB's foreign operations.

World News

This assassination had no political consequences; it was purely a demonstration of Stalin's revenge, and to show the world that no one could safely challenge his authority.

Marshal Tito
1953

In the 1940s and 1950s Stalin and Jozip Broz, known as Tito, the supreme ruler of Yugoslavia, became enemies. A letter from Tito found in a desk after Stalin's death carried this warning: 'Stop sending people to murder me. We have captured five of them with a bomb, and another a rifle . . . if you don't stop I will send a man to Moscow, and there'll be no need to send any more.'

Stalin chose Iosif Grigulevich to prepare the assassination of Tito.

This is the most extraordinary photograph in the history of assassination. The target and the assassin are having a friendly meeting, both smoking. Tito thinks he is meeting the Costa Rican chargé d'affaires, who is in fact the experienced Soviet assassin Iosif Grigulevich.

Grigulevich worked in Latin America and had created a new personality of himself as Teodoro Castro, securing his recognition as a chargé d'affaires of Costa Rica, first in Rome and then in Yugoslavia, which he visited for the first time in 1952. He was well received by Tito's staff and had a personal meeting with the President: as an experienced assassin, he knew that access to the target was essential. At a meeting in Vienna in 1953 with Stalin's officials various methods of assassination were discussed – pistol, poison or gas. A plan was sent to Stalin to read on 1 March 1953, but in the early hours of the next day Stalin suffered a fatal stroke and he died three days later. The idea of Tito's assassination was dropped, and Grigulevich returned to Moscow to develop an academic career for himself as an expert on South America.

THE PUTIN REGIME OF VENGEFUL DESPOTISM

Vladimir Putin served in the KGB, became head of its successor, the FSB, the Federal Security Service of the Russian Federation, and in 2000 became President of the Soviet Union. He continued in that position until 2008, was Prime Minister under Medvedev until 2012, and since then he has been President again. He proved himself to be Stalin's heir when in 2006 he asked a tame Duma to pass a law allowing the FSB to kill terrorists abroad. In Putin's Russia there is no free press and no rule of law, for the judges do what the Government tells them to do, and in foreign affairs it seeks to subvert elections in other countries that are liberal democracies. If necessary, violence is used, as in the Crimea and Ukraine and assassination on the streets of Britain, and then they lie about it. Both Putin and Trump characterise any criticism as 'fake news'. One of the main instruments of Putin's regime is the official use of targeted killings.

Russia's capacity to assassinate dissidents or traitors had increased significantly through the very large biological and chemical weapons programme in the many laboratories of Biopreparat. In 1979 there had been an outbreak of anthrax in the area; no independent report was published, as the Kremlin asserted that it was due to natural causes. Biopreparat was beginning to experiment with biological weapons, and one of the nerve agents it created was Novichok. The West only became aware of this through the defection to Britain in 1989 of one of Russia's scientific directors, Vladimir Pasechnik. Some of his revelations were so horrific that the information he provided has remained classified.

For their targeted killings, the FSB and the GRU, the Soviet military intelligence service, have used chemical and biological weapons. In 2004 they attempted to assassinate Viktor Yushchenko in the Ukrainian presidential election: they used dioxins, which disfigured him but did not kill him. For the Skripals in Salisbury they chose Novichok. In this century there have been secret assassinations by the FSB of the leaders of the various states that make up Chechnya: in 2004 the Deputy Prime Minister, in 2005 the Vice President of the area of Ichkeria, and in 2015 the Emir of the Caucasian Emirate and the Emir of Dagestan.

Putin has created a political and social atmosphere where any dissent is disloyal, and if people want to gain his favour they do what they think will please him. So Putin does not have to give his personal approval for each assassination of political opponents, investigative journalists, or exiled dissidents, as he knows there are many willing agents who will do his dirty work for him. When he agreed to the release in a prisoner exchange of Sergei Skripal, the convicted Russian double agent, his throwaway comment was 'We need another Mercader.' That was the twenty-first century version of 'Who will rid me of this turbulent priest?'

Viktor Yushchenko
5 September 2004

In the election for the presidency of the Ukraine in 2004 Viktor Yushchenko was seeking to defeat Viktor Yanukovych, who was supported by Putin. On 5 September he went for dinner with Ihor Smeshko, head of Ukraine's intelligence

Viktor Yushchenko suffering from chloracne caused by dioxin poisoning

service, and his deputy, Volodymyr Satsyuk, at the latter's house in Kiev. Later that evening he fell ill, and he was rushed to a hospital in Vienna. His wife was suspicious from the start: she had told him that his lips had tasted metallic when he kissed her on returning home. His body started to swell and his head grew much larger; slowly all his skin became inflamed and covered with pus. It was thought he would not survive. The hospital discovered that he had been poisoned with dioxin. Yushchenko thought it had been put in the rice in the dinner. He was not surprised to learn that his host had fled to Russia and been given Russian citizenship to avoid extradition to the Ukraine.

Yushchenko recovered sufficiently to fight the election, though to win he had to fight a second round, and was President of the Ukraine from 2005 to 2010. He had in fact survived a Russian assassination attempt. In 2018, reflecting upon the attempted murder of Sergei Skripal in Salisbury, he said: 'I am amazed that countries in Europe are so blind to the medieval policy that Russia follows in the twenty-first century. I feel pain for Europe.'

Boris Nemtsov
27 February 2015

As he was walking across the Bolshoy Moskvoretsky Bridge near the Kremlin with his fiancée after a dinner together, Boris Nemtsov was shot four times in his back. This was a well-planned assassination: the murderers must have penetrated his diary, followed him, and picked the moment when he was most vulnerable.

The Russian political system does not recognise the post of Leader of the Opposition, but if it had that would have been Nemtsov. Back in the early 1990s he had been the first Deputy Prime Minister under Boris Yeltsin, who looked upon him as his successor, but it was not to be. From that time he was involved in politics, and at the time of his murder he was co-chairman of the alliance of liberals and democrats. He had the personal courage to take on Putin, whom he had known when he was a member of the KGB. Nemtsov was charismatic, and

Boris Nemtsov, the victim, and the assassin

there are photographs of them shaking hands, though the President probably did not like him, being a head taller. In the Russian media Nemtsov was beginning to reveal the widespread corruption of the Putin machine, particularly what involved embezzlement and profiteering ahead of the Olympics in Sochi, the town where Nemtsov was born.

The other policy, entirely driven forward by Putin himself, was the annexation of the Crimea and the deployment of Soviet troops to sustain the fighting in the eastern Ukraine. Nemtsov, engaged in compiling a report on Russian troops in the Ukraine whose presence Putin continued to deny, was not going to pull any punches: 'This is not our war, it is not your war, this is not the war of twenty-year-old paratroopers sent out there. It is Vladimir Putin's war.' Putin had had enough, and Nemtsov was killed just two days before a great anti-corruption meeting and march. That went ahead in spite of his murder.

In July 2017 five men from Chechnya, led by Zaur Dadayev, were found guilty of Nemtsov's murder and given prison sentences ranging from twenty to

Putin with his assassination buddy Ramzan Kadyrov, head of the Chechen Republic

eleven years, which were thought to be light. They all protested their innocence. At no time during the trial was there an attempt to identify the persons who paid them. Nemtsov's lawyers and friends claimed that the assassination had been organised by Ramzan Kadyrov, the autocratic dictator of the Chechen Republic and a close personal friend of Putin, who on an earlier occasion had described Dadayev as a patriot.

There was absolutely no chance that at the next election Nemtsov could have defeated Putin, who knew, having been brought up in the old Soviet Communist days, how to fix an election. But this assassination achieved two things: the silencing of Putin's most effective critic, and a warning of what would happen to anybody who dared to challenge him. The line of responsibility will never be traced back to the President, but the world recognises that one of the ways in which Putin secures his supremacy is by state-sponsored assassination.

On 14 December 2017 at a press conference attended by 1,640 reporters Putin announced his candidacy for the presidential election. Barefacedly he deplored the absence of any opposition, asking: 'Is it up to me to form the opposition myself?' One opposition candidate who is still alive is the thirty-six-year-old TV presenter Ksenia Sobchak; she was bold enough to say: 'People understand that being an opposition figure in Russia means either you get killed or jailed, or something like that.' Boris Nemtsov had been shot two years earlier; Alexei Navalny announced his candidacy a year later, but he was barred from standing by a trumped-up conviction for fraud. His brother was also jailed, on another fraud charge, and his supporters are frequently harassed by the police.

Peter Brookes, *The Times*, 15 December 2017

Sergei Skripal
4 March 2018

One Sunday in the quiet cathedral town of Salisbury an elderly man and a younger woman were found slumped together on a park bench. The woman looked as if she was unconscious, but a passerby said that the man was doing 'some strange hand movements looking up to the sky'. A member of the public called the police at 4:15pm. It transpired that the man was Sergei Skripal, who had been a Soviet spy working as a double agent for Britain, and the woman was his daughter, who was visiting him from Russia. He had been trained as a soldier, but had joined the GRU in the 1980s at a time when it was thought to be more efficient than the KGB. While serving in Spain he became an agent for Britain's MI6, passing secret information for a payment of $3,000 a meeting. In 2000 he retired as a colonel, but in 2004 he was arrested in Russia, charged with treason, and sentenced to thirteen years in jail.

In 2010, in the biggest spy swap since the Cold War, ten Soviet agents were

Sergei and Yulia Skripal

returned to Russia in exchange for two sent to America and two to Britain. Skripal was one of those who came to Britain. In 2011 he bought a house in a cul-de-sac in Salisbury for £350,000 in cash. His neighbours said he was friendly and usually wore a tracksuit. They also knew that his wife and son had both died in strange circumstances in recent years.

The hospital had no idea what had caused Skripal and his daughter to become so seriously ill. They owe their lives to the fact that Porton Down, the British laboratory developing chemical weapons and their antidotes, was just down the road: it knew about Novichok and the treatment that could neutralise it. In the hospital the Skripals were treated with a mixture of atropine (an anti-convulsant which stabilises the effect of the nerve agent on the muscles) and oxime (which breaks down the neurotransmitter, acetylcholine, that increases nerve agents to a lethal level). One of the police officers, Detective Sergeant Nick Bailey, who had been early on the scene examining the two victims, also suffered from the poison, and was in a serious condition in hospital. In her statement to the House of Commons, Theresa May said they had been poisoned by a nerve agent called

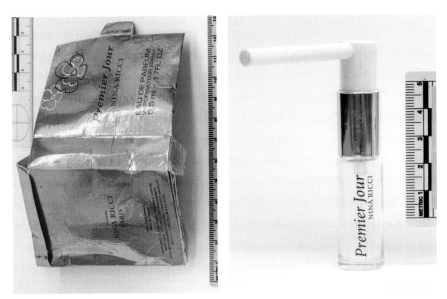

The packaging and the scent bottle

Novichok which had been developed in Russia in the 1970s. She continued: 'If it was clear that Russia had used a nerve agent to murder someone in Britain then action will be taken.' The Russian Foreign Minister scoffed at this, but not when Mrs May announced later than twenty-three Russia diplomats were to be expelled. Donald Trump followed suit, as did twenty other countries in the European Union including Estonia and Lithuania. Detective Sergeant Bailey was able to leave hospital within a week, and Sergei's daughter, Yulia, regained consciousness, leaving hospital five weeks later to stay at a protected secret address. She declined to meet Russian officials, and the Embassy declared that she had been abducted. After twelve weeks in the Salisbury hospital Sergei was allowed to leave to join his daughter in their secret safe house. Putin greeted this news by saying that as they had both recovered they could not have been poisoned by a nerve agent – a new official line.

On 30 June in Amesbury, just a few miles from Salisbury, a couple, Charlie Rowley and Dawn Sturgess, were found to be suffering from the effects of a nerve agent, and they were rushed to the hospital in Salisbury that had saved the Skripals. Novichok was identified as the cause. Charlie was discharged after three weeks, but his partner Dawn died without recovering consciousness. Charlie told the police that he had found a box containing a scent bottle which he gave to Dawn as a present and she had sprayed it on her wrists, but within fifteen minutes she had begun to fall ill. The Soviet agents were reckless and stupid to throw away the bottle of Novichok, since it would be found by someone and would provide more clues to their operation. So a poisoned scent bottle joins the list of a poisoned cup of tea and a poisoned umbrella as assassination weapons.

In July the US State Department to everyone's surprise imposed sanctions on Russia because a chemical weapon had been used in Salisbury. In American law sanctions are the automatic consequence when chemical or biological weapons are used. Russia immediately complained that this was illegal and disproportionate, but President Trump's reaction was complete silence, not even one Tweet, as he had arranged a meeting with Putin and did not want to precede it with a warlike move.

The two assassins at Salisbury Station

In September 2018 Theresa May announced to Parliament that the security services and the police had identified the two Russian assassins who had attempted to kill the Skripals. They were Alexander Petrov and Ruslan Boshirov, though these were thought to be false names, and both were members of the GRU. The evidence to back this up was devastating. CCTV images tracked the pair arriving at Gatwick at 3.00pm on 2 March, then staying at a small two-star hotel in the East End of London. On 3 March they went on a dummy run in Salisbury. On 4 March they arrived in Salisbury at 11.48am and were seen walking close to Skripal's house at 1.05pm. Finally they left from Heathrow at 7.28pm. Never before have assassins been so visually recorded. The Prime Minister also said: 'This was not a rogue operation and almost certainly approved at a senior level in the Russian state.'

The two assassins made careless mistakes. To leave no tracks they should have travelled separately on different routes; worn hoods rather than baseball caps or woollen hats; stayed at two different hotels; and not be seen walking together in Salisbury. Above all, they should not have thrown away the scent bottle. This was poor spycraft and brazen over-confidence, almost as if they did not care if they were found out, for they were beyond the normal rules of moral behaviour. Ben Wallace, the British Security Minister, commented: 'This was more Johnny English than James Bond.'

The Skripal assassination took an even more bizarre turn when early in September 2018 Putin announced that the two accused Russians had been tracked down and as they were civilians they would appear on television to tell their story. On 13 September the West learnt from the TV interview that they were nutrition experts who went as tourists to see Salisbury Cathedral, especially its 125-metre spire, and Old Sarum. No questions were allowed about their previous lives, or where their factories or homes were. There was no CCTV evidence of them visiting the Cathedral, but they had been filmed about a mile away from Salisbury Station and a visit to Old Sarum would have required a return walk of one hour. This was a ludicrous pantomime, and the world was amazed at the humiliation that Putin had inflicted upon two incompetent spies who had let down their country.

MI6 had been tracking GRU's activities for some time. In 1963 when GRU discovered that Oleg Penkovsky, a senior officer, was passing secrets to MI6 they strapped him to a stretcher and cremated him alive, and filmed his death as a warning to others. GRU were responsible for many attacks in the Ukraine and Syria, and played a pivotal role in the annexation of the Crimea by seizing vital installations. In all probability it was a GRU officer who shot down the Malaysia Airlines Flight 17 over the Ukraine in 2014. They were also involved in the cyber-attacks in the 2016 US presidential election which were so damaging to Hillary Clinton. They had a long record of extreme violence and had become a law unto themselves, and in the case of Sergei Skripal they condemned to death a GRU officer who had been a traitor.

Russia's team of assassins came a cropper over the Skripal case, for the victims survived and the assassins were filmed. A Peter Brookes cartoon published

Peter Brookes, *The Times*, 9 March 2018

on 9 March 2018 depicts Putin's reaction to the press of the world which has accepted that Russia was responsible; the pictures on the wall behind him recall the murders of the investigative journalists Litvinenko and Markov (see below).

In May 2018 Andrew Parker, the head of MI5, speaking to a meeting of security chiefs in Berlin, said that the Salisbury incident was a 'deliberate and targeted malign activity' which made Russia 'a more isolated pariah'. As the Russians had flooded their tame media services and social media with a mass of conspiracy theories, Parker said he was glad to 'shine a light through the fog of lies, half-truths and obfuscations that pour out of their propaganda machine'.

In September 2018 a company in Leicester called Bellingcat, helped by an investigative website in Russia, Insider, revealed that the failed assassin Boshirov was in fact Colonel Anatoliy Chepiga, an officer of the GRU, who had received from Putin in 2014 Russia's top military honour. They tracked down his place of birth as the village of Nikolayeka in Eastern Siberia, and the BBC managed to find a Russian woman who confirmed that she recognised Chepiga by his voice. Once again, the whole operation was shown up to be sloppy and careless. Their two passports carried marks reserved only for intelligence agents. Bellingcat published a photograph of Chepiga as a younger man alongside the CCTV pictures. The editor of the Insider news site, Roman Dobrokhotov, who had done much of the local digging and interviewing, expects to be arrested or possibly have his bank account closed. One of the leading journalists working for Insider, Sergei Kanev, fled the country, believing that he was about to be arrested and framed for plotting to assassinate President Putin.

In October the ever resourceful Bellingcat revealed that the second assassin, who had used the pseudonym Alexander Petrov, was in fact Alexander Mishkin, a doctor working for the GRU. His passport from 2001 was recovered: his registered home address in Moscow was the GRU headquarters.

In February 2019 Bellingcat revealed that a third Soviet agent, Sergei Fedutov, had entered Britain two days before the attack on the Skripals. In the past Fedutov had travelled under the name Denis Sergeev; he was thought to have been involved in a botched nerve agent attack on an arms dealer in Bulgaria, Emiliyan Gebrev.

According to a report by King's College London in 2019, the Russian state broadcaster RT and the news agency Sputnik spread seven different conspiracy theories on the Skirpal attack involving 138 contradictory accounts deliberately to create confusion.

Revelations after the Skripal attempt

As a consequence of the Skripal attempted assassination the Home Secretary, Amber Rudd, announced an inquiry to be led by the Metropolitan Police Counter-Terrorism Command into whether any of the fourteen deaths of named Russians over the last two decades could be traced back to the Kremlin. Two of the most significant were as follows:

* Boris Berezovsky, an oligarch who fell out with Putin and had been given asylum in Britain despite fraud charges, was found dead in 2013. His death was consistent with hanging by a scarf from his shower-rail.
* Badr Patarkatsishvili, a close friend of Berezovsky, had died in 2008, having expressed concern that four Georgians had been sent 'to do something against me'.

A further followed. Nikolai Glushkov was a friend of Berezovsky and a deputy director of Aeroflot, which he claimed in 1999 was acting as 'a cash cow to support

Glushkov, Berezovsky and Patarkatsishvili – all dead

international spying operations'. He was given a three-year sentence. In 2010 he was granted asylum in Britain. He was found dead on 12 March 2018, a week after the attack on Skripal, in his flat in New Malden. He had been strangled.

Alexander Zakharchenko
31 August 2018

In February 2014 there was a spontaneous uprising in the Ukraine to overthrow the corrupt government of President Yanukovych, which was heavily dependent on the support of Russia and President Putin. A pro-Western government was quickly established. The eastern province of the Ukraine which bordered Russia started a separatist movement: in April rebel militants, of whom one of the leading members was Alexander Zakharchenko, took over control of the main administrative buildings in Donetsk, the major town, and sought independence from Kiev. After a referendum on the issue of sovereignty and a general election, which many believe was rigged, a parliament emerged which appointed Zakharchenko as Prime Minister of the Donetsk People's Republic. For the following four years there was a civil war in which over 10,000 people were killed; the Russians, although they denied it, provided extensive military help. Zakharchenko had supported the Minsk deal which sought a negotiated settlement in which Germany, France and Russia were engaged.

On 31 August Zakharchenko was killed by a bomb placed in a popular war-themed restaurant in Donetsk. Russia immediately called this a terrorist attack organised by the Ukrainian Government, which not surprisingly denied it. Assassination was not a novelty in the People's Republic: in 2016 a Russian-born commander, Arsen Pavlov nicknamed Motorola, was killed by a bomb in his lift, and in 2017 another rebel commander was killed by a rocket fired into his office. There had been seven targeted killings, attributed by the West to rivalries between various local militias. For the assassins to know exactly when Zakharchenko was going to be in the local café they must have had access to his diary.

It is by no means clear who killed him. The Russians accused the government

The funeral of the rebel leader

in Kiev, but that is highly unlikely, as Zakharchenko was engaged in peace negotiations involving France, Germany, Russia and the Ukraine. It is much more likely that Putin wanted him removed because Russia was uncomfortable with the fact that Paris and Berlin were involved in matters which they considered to be internal. On the day of the assassination Russia's Foreign Minister said: 'Talks involving Kiev, Moscow, Berlin and Paris are currently impossible.' This killing can only create great instability, which may well suit Russia.

The Russian Ambassador to Turkey, Andrei Karlov, shot dead at a photographic exhibition in Ankara by an off-duty Turkish policeman in December 2016

When it comes to assassination, Russia does not always have it its own way. Turkey had protested very strongly at Putin's support for Assad's forces which had razed Aleppo in Syria to the ground, killing many Muslims. In December 2016 the Russian Ambassador to Turkey, Andrei Karlov, had been asked to open a photographic exhibition in Ankara. There he was shot by an off-duty Turkish policeman, who shouted 'Do not forget Aleppo.' The assassin was himself shot dead by Turkish police. This was Russia's poisoned chalice. Those who engage in assassinations can themselves be targets.

IV

AUSTRO-HUNGARIAN EMPIRE & GERMANY

'I would not be surprised if over there a couple of Serbian bullets were waiting for me.'

ARCHDUKE FRANZ FERDINAND

Archduke Franz Ferdinand
28 June 1914

The heir to the Austro-Hungarian Empire, Archduke Franz Ferdinand, and his wife Sophie, Duchess of Hohenberg, were shot dead by a Bosnian assassin in Sarajevo, the capital of Bosnia, on 28 June 1914. The Archduke had spent the previous few days asserting the military power of the Austrian Army by observing military manoeuvres in Bosnia, which had been annexed to the Austro-Hungarian Empire as recently as 1908. The largest ethnic group in Bosnia, approaching half of the population, were Serbians (a third were Muslims and a quarter were Croatians). A secret society, Young Bosnia, campaigned for Bosnia to be absorbed into neighbouring Serbia. It found an ally in a group in Serbia called the Black Hand, consisting of dissident army officers, with the campaigning cry of 'Union or Death'. Colonel Dragutin Dimitrijevic, the chief of Serbian military intelligence, nicknamed 'Apis' after the sacred bull of Egyptian mythology, was the leader of the Black Hand. At his trial in 1917, when he was accused of plotting to kill the Crown Prince of Serbia, he claimed that he had masterminded the Sarajevo assassination, although previously he had denied any knowledge of it. This attempt to show his Serbian patriotism did not work: he was found guilty and executed.

It was assumed that the Serbian Government had planned and executed the assassination of the Archduke, and therefore it was responsible for lighting the spark that led to the First World War. The latest book about the assassination, *Folly and Malice* by a Serbian historian, John Zametica, after a most scrupulous

Major Vojislav Tankosić

scholarly and extensive search of all the relevant records, memoirs, official reports, hundreds of eyewitness statements and recordings of trials in Serbia, Russia and Bosnia, came to the conclusion that Apis did not mastermind the assassination.

What cannot be disputed is that three Bosnian students went to Belgrade in the spring of 1914 and were given weapons, bombs, grenades and Browning pistols by a hot-headed, violent maverick Serbian officer who was also a member

of the Black Hand, Major Vojislav Tankosić, who had also arranged some firing practice for them. In the Balkans at the beginning of the twentieth century being a student was synonymous with being a socialist, a radical and a revolutionary.

The three students – Gavrilo Princip, Nedeljko Čabrinović, and Trifko Grabež – had met in 1913 and agreed that Franz Ferdinand, the heir to the Austro-Hungarian Empire, was 'an enemy of the Slavs'. When they learnt he was to visit Sarajevo they decided to kill him. Their purpose was to detach Bosnia from that Empire and unite it to Serbia to create

Gavrilo Princip

a Greater Serbian state. At his trial Princip was asked how Bosnia could be freed from Austria and then allowed to join Serbia. His reply was: 'By Terror . . . killing people at the top, removing those evil-doers standing in the way and hindering the idea of unification'. He saw himself as a Bosnian nationalist terrorist, passionately devoted to freeing Bosnia from Austria's colonial rule, and it was that passion, combined with his hatred of Austria, that sustained him over many long months.

As soon as they returned to Bosnia Princip set about recruiting four more assassins. He turned to a longstanding friend and former teacher, Danilo Ilić.

Ilić introduced him to a Muslim Serb, a carpenter, Muhamed Mehmedbašić, who had earlier volunteered to engage in the assassination of the Governor of Bosnia, Oskar Potiorek (that was abandoned). The sixth was Vaso Čubrilović, a seventeen-year-old student. The seventh was Cvjetko Popović, a radical student from Croatia.

Franz Ferdinand and his wife were to arrive by train and then travel in an open car (his ADC had asked for a covered car) which had been lent by a personal friend, Count Harrach, down a long straight road, Apple Quay, which ran alongside the Miljacka River for about four miles to reach the Town Hall. This came to be known as 'The Avenue of the Assassins'.

The Archduke was in full sky-blue parade uniform of a cavalry general, with a helmet with its distinctive plume of pale green ostrich feathers: he was, after all, wanting to emphasise the military power of the Austro-Hungarian Empire. He and his wife joined a motorcade of eight cars of which his was the third. His fellow passengers were Governor Potiorek and Harrach. The seven assassins were allocated separate positions along the route. It is strange that the first position was assigned to the youngest and least experienced, Čubrilović, who had received no weapons training, and said later, 'When I saw the Archduke I felt troubled about killing him.'

The second assassin was Čabrinović, who was armed only with a bomb; as the car passed he detonated it by slamming it on a lamppost and tossed it over the car where it landed on the folded roof, bounced off, and rolled under the following car. The bomb was filled with nails and chopped lead: it hurt two children and severely injured Colonel Merrizzi, the ADC of the Governor, who as an enthusiastic supporter of the visit had argued very strongly only on the previous evening that the visit should not be cancelled on security grounds. Čabrinović tried to get away by jumping into the river, but he was soon arrested by the police who had to fight off a lynch mob that was beginning to assault him. When Franz Ferdinand saw this he remarked to Potiorek, 'Why don't the security men allow those people to club him to death! The Court will as usual only condemn him to four or five years, and then furthermore soon pardon him.'

A black-and-white photograph of Franz Ferdinand coloured by the Brazilian artist Marina Aramal, the leading expert in colouring historical photographs. It was published in 2018

Not a policeman in sight

The third assassin, just thirty paces away, was Mehmedbašić; he could have thrown his bomb at the motorcade, but he decided to retreat to a safer position. The fourth was Popović, who was short-sighted and out of vanity refused to wear glasses. He was not cut out to be an assassin, and said later: 'I lacked the energy to do it. I do not know why I lacked it.' The sixth assassin, Grabež, with a Browning revolver in his pocket, was persuaded by Ilić not to fire on the cars as they drove slowly by. By the time the Archduke had reached the Town Hall six of the assassins had failed.

In the Town Hall Franz Ferdinand stopped the Mayor making his welcome speech, thundering: 'This is outrageous, a disgrace, bombs have been thrown. Is that what one comes to Sarajevo for?' He then decided that he would like to visit the wounded Merrizzi in hospital, which meant that a different route would be needed, and with this he signed his own death warrant. Halfway along the Apple Quay the motorcade would have to turn right into Franz Joseph Street and pass through narrower streets to reach the hospital. Potiorek devised a plan whereby the two first cars in the motorcade would turn right, acting as decoys, and the remainder, led by the Archduke's car, would carry on driving down the straight and safer Apple Quay. This led Potiorek to assure Franz Ferdinand, 'Your Imperial Highness can drive safely. I take the responsibility.'

However several key people did not have his plan explained to them – not even Harrach, who had decided to protect the Archduke by standing on the runningboard of his car. The Commissioner of Police travelling in the first car and the driver of the second were told by Potiorek to turn right into Franz Joseph Street. The driver of the Archduke's car, Lojka, said he was only told to follow the car in front. So when the two first cars turned right he followed. Immediately Potiorek realised this was a mistake and ordered Lojka to reverse, which meant that for some precious moments the car was stopped.

Gavrilo Princip was waiting on the river side of Apple Quay. When he saw the first two cars turning into Franz Joseph Street he quickly crossed over to where it was less crowded, and was just six feet away from the stopped car. Later he said: 'So I drew the revolver and raised it towards the car without aiming. As I shot I even turned my head away.' His first bullet hit the back door and passed through a sheet of aluminium, the wooden construction and the leather upholstery before entering the lower abdomen of the Duchess, severing her main artery. Princip's second unaimed shot was also a fluke. He held the revolver in one hand and its recoil forced the gun higher; at that moment he just pulled the trigger without aiming. The bullet passed through the Archduke's neck, severing both the jugular vein and the carotid artery. If it had followed a trajectory just one inch away, the Archduke would not have been hit. As the shots were unaimed it was pure chance that each was so fatal. Within two hours both the Archduke and Duchess were dead. Princip swallowed a cyanide capsule; it did not work, so he attempted to shoot himself, but the police stopped him.

The lack of security on the day was amazing. Sarajevo had a police force of 112, but they don't appear in any of the photographs. They were not lining the route, and when the Archduke left the Town Hall the only people surrounding him were council officials. There were no soldiers in the town. The photograph taken of the Archduke's car just before it made its fatal decision to turn right

The Archduke's car on Apple Quay before turning into Franz Joseph Street.
Where's the security?

shows that it seems to be driving almost alone with the following car barely in sight, and there are no police to be seen.

The best advice heard that day in the Town Hall was from an officer, Major Paul Höger, who had suggested that the party should stay in the Town Hall until Austrian soldiers had entered Sarajevo and cleared the streets. If his advice had been taken the First World War would not have broken out in August 1914. However Potiorek dismissed it, on the grounds that the soldiers would be in their field uniforms and thus unsuitable for lining the streets. The troops reached Sarajevo by 3.00pm, four hours after the assassination.

The aged Emperor Franz Joseph saw the assassination as a direct threat to the authority of the Austro-Hungarian Empire. He did not want his Hapsburg Empire to disintegrate like the Ottoman Empire, its neighbour to the south, so

Serbia's ambition had to be stopped. The Emperor sent a handwritten letter to the Kaiser, Wilhelm II: 'The existing peace policies of all European Monarchs will be at risk so long as the furnace of criminal agitation in Belgrade continues to burn unpunished.' In a week Germany gave its 'blank cheque' to Austria, the Kaiser scribbling a note on the official document: 'The Serbs must be disposed of and that right soon.' Austria issued a humiliating ultimatum to Serbia which the Serbian Government accepted in virtually all its terms, apart from one which gave Austria the right to interfere in Serbia's internal affairs. That exemption gave Austria the excuse to break off diplomatic relations immediately, and on 28 July it declared war on Serbia. Russia mobilised to defend the Slavs, and Churchill mobilised the British Navy. On 4 August Britain declared war on Germany for its invasion of Belgium. Bosnia and Serbia were soon forgotten.

Just thirty-five days after this assassination in a Balkan backwater all the major countries in Europe – France, Germany, Britain, Russia and Austria – were engaged in a war that was to change the history of the world. How could there be a direct causal link between small Balkan states and a world war? Many historians have traced everything that happened in all of those countries during those thirty-five days to try to determine how it happened, and they have come to many different conclusions.

My tutor at Oxford, A. J. P. Taylor, in a brilliant series of lectures on the First World War asserted that 'there were no causes to the War, it just happened'. This is to say that even if the Sarajevo assassination had not happened the build-up of large armies and fleets by all the main European countries created tensions, particularly through Germany's imperial ambitions, that could only be resolved by conflict. Others however did recognise a direct causal link, and one of those was Harold Macmillan. I remember one evening in the early 1980s after a dinner at the Carlton Club where he had been speaking to a small gathering; I was standing next to him at the window of the Club's drawing room, on the first floor looking down on St James's Street, and in a mellow and reflective mood, never one to miss a dramatic moment, he said:

I was standing at this window at the end of a sunny day in June 1914 when I saw a paperboy in the street below carrying a placard strapped on a board around his waist bearing the words, 'Murder of Austrian Arch-Duke'. Little did I think that this news would lead within little more than a month to a war that would change the history of the world and would also lead to the death of so many of my friends.

The Balkans were the spark that involved Germany as a supporter of the Austro-Hungarian Empire, and Russia as a supporter of Serbia, making it impossible to limit the assassination to an internal affair of Eastern Europe.

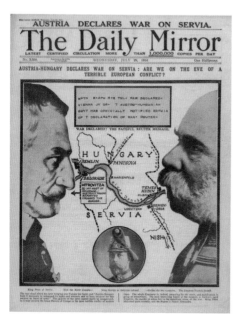

The *Daily Mirror* of 28 July 1914 could barely conceive that a war between King Peter I of Serbia, whom no one had heard of, and the aged Emperor Franz Joseph of Austria, who had been born before Queen Victoria ascended the throne, could lead to a terrible European conflict.

THE NAZIS

Ernst Röhm
1 July 1934

'If I am going to be killed let Adolf do it himself.'

Ernst Röhm, a former soldier, in the early 1920s became a political ally and a close friend of Hitler, indeed so close that he alone was allowed to call him 'Adolf'. In the rise of Nazism he was the one who recruited ex-soldiers to form an unofficial army of fighting thugs, dressed in brown shirts and known as the SA (Storm Battalion). These stormtroopers initiated street battles with 'Reds' and Jews, intimidating anyone who opposed them.

In 1931 he reorganised the SA to make it even more powerful, since he looked upon it as an instrument for constant revolution. That was something that Hitler no longer wanted. Both the army and influential businessmen who funded Nazism looked upon Röhm as a real threat: his SA had become a very large force of one million men, and Röhm had plans for it to take over the German Army. Hitler certainly did not want that. With his closest henchmen,

Hitler and Röhm, when they were friends

Himmler and Goering, Hitler drew up a list of the officers and staff of the Brown Shirts who had to be assassinated in the 'Night of the Long Knives' from 30 June to 2 July 1934. The estimates of those who were summarily killed vary from 400 to over 1,000. Hitler justified it by saying that Röhm was planning a coup.

He had ordered that when Röhm was captured he was to be put in a prison cell with a loaded revolver. When Röhm realised he was not going to get out alive, he said: 'If I am going to be killed let Adolf do it himself.' He opened the cell door, stripped to the waist, and stood to attention. Two SS officers shot him at point-blank range. Hitler ordered that two generals should also be killed, to show the army that they also had to owe him undivided loyalty.

Adolf Hitler: the Beer Hall Putsch
8 November 1939

When the Second World War broke out in 1939 Hitler was very lucky to escape being assassinated in a beer cellar in Munich.

Some generals and senior civil servants, appalled by the bestiality of the invasion of Poland, were considering ways to stop Hitler from launching a war against France and Britain, but they lacked the will and determination to take on his outright dominance and unassailable position. He could only be destroyed by a coup d'état or an assassination. One man, unknown to them and unknown to the Gestapo, had decided to kill him. This was George Elser, a thirty-six-year-old joiner from Schwabia. He had no political motive and no special way of getting close to Hitler, but he was very concerned about the anger of workers at their conditions and how those would get worse if there were to be a war. He decided the only way to prevent a war was to kill the Führer.

Elser learnt from newspapers that Hitler was going to speak on 8 November in the famous Bürgerbräukeller in Munich, where the Nazi movement had started on that day in 1923. In the summer and autumn he visited the beer cellar several times, and discovered that Hitler would make his speech from a platform, standing in front of a wooden pillar. Elser planned to conceal a time bomb in the pillar, and spent several nights hollowing it out. He also stole explosives and dynamite from the company he worked for and tested out explosions in his parents' garden. He managed to place the bomb inside the pillar a day before the meeting.

Hitler's annual speech usually started at 8.30pm and was followed by drinks for the faithful, ending at 10 o'clock. On this occasion he started at 8:10pm with a tirade against Britain and finished at 9.07pm. He then decided not to stay for drinks with the 'Old Fighters' but leave immediately for Berlin to deal with the

Hitler speaking in the Bürgerbräukeller, 8 November 1939

French attack on the Saarland. At 9.20pm, thirteen minutes after Hitler had left, the bomb was detonated, killing 8 and injuring 63 others.

In the meantime Elser planned to get to Switzerland, but at the time of the explosion he was under arrest on the Swiss border as he had tried to cross it illegally. When the border guards found in his pockets a postcard of the beer cellar they put two and two together, realising he must have had a hand in the attempted murder of Hitler which they had just been hearing about on the radio. Hitler initially wanted a show trial to incriminate the British Secret Service, but instead Elser was held in the concentration camp at Dachau for five years, and shortly before the Americans liberated that camp he was shot by the Gestapo.

If this assassination had been successful it would have changed the history of the world. The generals, many of whom were opposed to the war, might have seized the opportunity to eliminate the clique around Hitler – Goebbels, Goering and Himmler. Even if they did not do that, there was no Nazi who could replace the passion and willpower of the Führer. The war against France and Britain was essentially Hitler's personal war: without Hitler at the helm it might never have happened.

The failure of Elser's plan made Hitler totally impregnable and made his 'solution only with the sword' inevitable. In his speech on 23 November to two hundred generals he said:

> I must in all modesty describe my own person: irreplaceable. Neither a military man nor a civilian could replace me. Attempts at assassination may be repeated. I am convinced of my powers of intellect and decision. Wars are always ended by the annihilation of the opponent. Anyone who believes differently is irresponsible.

Reinhard Heydrich
27 May 1942

Reinhard Heydrich was one of Hitler's closest henchmen in promoting the Holocaust, and he was seen by some as the Führer's possible successor. He had started his career in the German Navy, rising to lieutenant by 1931, but he was discharged on account of the many affairs he had. Then, persuaded by his wife – a member of the Nazi Party – he applied for a post with Himmler, who appointed him to establish an intelligence service in Munich that became a machine of terror and intimidation.

Heydrich rose quickly through the Nazi ranks, being appointed head of the Gestapo by Himmler in 1934. One of his first tasks was to destroy the power of Röhm, who was shot without trial and his followers were purged. The Gestapo had powers of arbitrary arrest which could not be challenged in court, and Heydrich used this to arrest and kill thousands of people. In the programme of 9–10 November 1938, known as 'Kristallnacht' (the Night of Glass), it was Heydrich who instructed all the police services across Germany not to intervene to stop the burning of synagogues, the smashing of the windows of Jewish shops, and the breaking in and looting that followed. By this time he had created a huge network of spies and informers to eliminate any opposition to Nazi supremacy. In 1941 he was made Protector of Bohemia and Moravia, parts of Czechoslovakia which had been incorporated into the Reich in 1935. On his appointment he said: 'We will Germanise the Czech vermin.' He set about destroying Czech culture and customs, and by early 1942 over 5,000 people had been sent to their deaths in concentration camps. He was known as 'The Butcher of Prague'.

He was one of the principal authors of the Holocaust, for in 1942 he chaired the infamous Wannsee Conference that agreed the Final Solution, which was to exterminate all Jews in Europe. He was brutal, despotic, merciless, and responsible for the mass movement of Jews from Poland, Czechoslovakia, Holland and Norway. Even Hitler recognised 'that man has a heart of iron'.

Reinhard Heydrich

The Czech Government in exile in London decided that Heydrich must be killed. A plan was developed with the help of the British Special Operations Executive (SOE) to parachute into Czechoslovakia two Czech freedom fighters, Josef Gabčík and Jan Krubs, on 28 December 1941, using a Handley Page aircraft. They spent five months carefully studying all the movements made by Heydrich and decided that their best chance was on his daily drive from his palace twelve miles outside the capital to his headquarters in Prague, Hradčany Castle. They noticed that he was very careless about his own security, never travelling with guards or a follow-up vehicle. There was a sharp hairpin bend in the road, and they decided to make their attempt at that point on 27 May 1942. As they expected, Heydrich was in his grey Mercedes open car seated next to the driver. As it slowed down,

The hole made by the grenade that killed Heydrich

Gabčík stepped forward and fired a sten gun, but it jammed. Instead of telling his driver to pull away quickly, Heydrich tried to kill the gunman. That provided the opportunity for the second assassin to lob a grenade at the side of the car, blowing a great hole and forcing fine splinters of steel, horsehair and leather into the lower back and spleen of Heydrich. It did not kill him instantly; he tried to fire at the gunmen, as Krubs escaped on a bicycle and Gabčík disappeared in the crowd and on to a tram.

The doctors at first were confident that Heydrich would recover, and Himmler visited him on 2 June to congratulate him. Heydrich recited lines from one of his father's operas:

The world is just a barrel organ which the Lord God turns himself.
We all have to dance to the tune that is already on the drum.

Hitler saluting the coffin of his protégé

For him the dance was with death. Two days later he succumbed to septic poisoning. He was given a state funeral in Berlin which Hitler himself attended.

The consequences of this assassination were appalling. The two assassins were betrayed by another freedom fighter for a large monetary reward (the betrayer was hanged after the war), and following a siege in the crypt of the church in which they were hiding they committed suicide. Over 13,000 Czechs were arrested, deported, imprisoned or executed. Hitler's revenge for his beloved Heydrich led to the worst atrocity of the Second World War. The whole village of Lidice was razed to the ground; all the men over fifteen, amounting to 173, were executed, and 195 women were sent to concentration camps. Many of the 70 children also perished. The small village of Ležáky was given similar treatment. The scheme for the mass killing of Polish Jews and dissidents, with three death camps at Belzec, Sobibor and Treblinka, was renamed 'Operation Reinhard' in his memory.

The Lidice Massacre

It was said of this assassination that the Czech Government in exile in London had wanted to show that their freedom fighters could engage in operations to undermine Nazi power, and to persuade the Czech people not to make peace with Germany. It had the reverse effect: it was a gamble that did not pay off. Heydrich's assassination was definitely a poisoned chalice.

Adolf Hitler: the Generals' Plot
20 July 1944

By the summer of 1944 a group of generals and senior officers had become convinced that Germany was going to lose the war. On 3 June the Allies had taken Rome; on 8 June 156,000 British, American and Canadian soldiers had successfully landed in France; the Russian Army was pushing the German Army back through Poland and would soon reach the German border; and every night Berlin was heavily bombed. They knew that Hitler would never surrender or negotiate a peace, so they decided that he should be killed.

Colonel Claus von Stauffenberg, the driving force behind the conspiracy to kill Hitler, came from an old aristocratic family. He had supported National Socialism for its belief in a strong army; he had been very impressed with Germany's conquest of Poland and the defeat of France, and for his courage he had been awarded the German Cross in gold. He had been badly wounded, losing his right eye, his right hand and two of the fingers on his left hand. However he found the massacre of Ukrainian Jews by the SS so appalling that he was convinced that Hitler should be removed. He was the coordinator of various attempts to kill Hitler, and also the author of a much broader plan, called Valkyrie, involving many senior officers who would organise the coup to take over the state after Hitler's death.

From autumn 1943 there were several plans with fellow conspirators or officers who were able to gain access to Hitler, but they all failed. In December a fellow conspirator was prepared to blow himself up together with Hitler with a grenade while Hitler was visiting a display of new uniforms, but this was abandoned when the uniforms were destroyed in an air raid. An

Colonel Claus Schenk, Graf von Stauffenberg

attempt by a lieutenant in 1944 was abandoned when Hitler's visit to another display was cancelled. In March another officer armed with a Browning pistol planned to kill Hitler during a briefing meeting, but he was not allowed into the meeting. Hitler's luck had held out.

In July 1944 Stauffenberg was promoted to colonel and made Chief of Staff to General Fromm, the head of the Reserve Army, which meant he would have access to Hitler at briefing meetings. On 6 July he had his first chance to kill

Hitler, but there was no suitable opportunity. He hoped to do it on 11 July, but he held back as Himmler was not going to be present, because he wanted to kill both of them. On 16 July he was so involved in the briefing that he did not have time to prime the bomb. His next visit to the Wolf's Lair, Hitler's headquarters in eastern Prussia, was on 20 July. At the last moment the meeting was moved to a modern building rather than the concrete bunker, so any explosion was likely to be dissipated rather than contained. This time Stauffenberg took two time bombs in his briefcase. At lunch he slipped out to the toilets and with his adjutant, Lieutenant Haeften, he primed one of the bombs; as time was running out they could not prime the second. The briefcase bomb was timed to go off in half an hour.

Stauffenberg returned to the briefing room, where a place was found for him on Hitler's right, and they actually shook hands. He placed the briefcase under the table and left the meeting. He planned to get into a car as soon as possible, to get to an aircraft which would return him to Berlin so that he could put Valkyrie into action. The explosion was very loud, so Stauffenberg believed that Hitler was dead. In fact the bomb did kill four people and injured many more, but Hitler was hardly hurt – his eardrums were pierced, his right arm bruised, there were a few burns on his hands, and his trousers and long white underwear were burnt. He recovered quickly and insisted that his meeting that afternoon with Mussolini should go ahead. He was very proud to show him the ruins of the briefing room. Over a tea meeting in front of Mussolini, Ribbentrop and Dönitz, Hitler embarked on a thirty-minute tirade, with foam on his lips, vowing vengeance on all those who opposed him, and said they would be executed or sent to concentration camps. He screamed that providence had saved him again, chosen to make world history.

Stauffenberg in the meantime had started to implement Valkyrie, but the news soon reached him that Hitler was not dead. It was confirmed on the radio when Goebbels reported that the Führer was alive and would make a broadcast of his own that night. Stauffenberg was immediately suspected because of his disappearance, and he was quickly tracked down in Berlin and arrested by

Hitler shows Mussolini the bomb-wrecked room

General Fromm. Fromm had been one of the conspirators, but when he heard that Hitler was alive he decided to save his skin by arresting Stauffenberg and the three others with him, Lieutenant Werner von Haeften, Major-General Friedrich Olbricht, and Colonel Albrecht Mertz von Quirnheim. There was an immediate court martial that sentenced them to be shot, and they were taken out into the courtyard of the Ministry to be executed. Stauffenberg was the third to be shot; Haeften jumped in front of the firing squad trying to save his leader. As Stauffenberg died he shouted, 'Long live our sacred Germany'. The four bodies were hastily buried, but Himmler the following day ordered that they should be exhumed and burnt. Fromm did not save his skin: Hitler had him shot a year later.

Hitler's vengeance on the disloyal officers was vicious and relentless. He now saw the officer corps as an aristocratic, elitist bunch of traitors, the main reason for all the defeats that Germany suffered. Himmler was given the task of cleaning up the corps. General Beck, formerly Chief of the General Staff, and Lieutenant-General Henning von Tresckow, who had also tried to kill Hitler in 1943, both

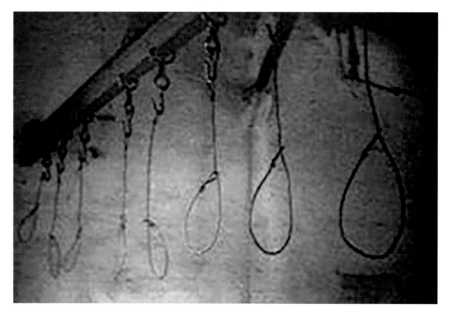

Eight of the plotters were executed by using piano wire to hang them slowly. Stauffenberg was lucky to be executed by firing squad

committed suicide on 21 July, as did Field-Marshal Kluge, the Commander in the Field. Carl-Heinrich von Stülpnagel, Commander of the forces in France, who had acted quickly to imprison the Gestapo in Paris, tried to shoot himself but only succeeded in blinding himself, so he was tried by the People's Court and condemned to be strangled. The purge continued, and a further 200 were executed. Hitler learnt that Rommel had known about the plot. He did not want him to be arrested and tried, for he was a national hero. He wanted him to commit suicide, and not by shooting himself, as the assumption in that case would be that Rommel was in on the plot. A messenger from Hitler told Rommel that if he took poison his death would be attributed to illness and he could have a state funeral with no repercussions for his family. That's what happened.

Hitler no longer trusted any generals, preferring officers from the Luftwaffe and the navy who still strongly supported him. For the army, this failed assassination was a poisoned chalice. Hitler wanted revenge and Himmler delivered it. 'Now I finally have the swine who have been sabotaging my work for years.' Over 5,000 people were arrested, tried without lawyers, and sentenced by a People's Court presided over by a fanatical Nazi. Hitler insisted that the traitors should be executed two hours after the sentence, with no religious rites, and hanged, not shot. 'Hanged. Hung up like meat carcasses.'

Eight officers were taken to a small room in a prison where there were eight meat hooks hanging from the ceiling. Each was stripped to the waist and hung up by a noose made of piano wire, which extended their death throes. The victims' trousers were removed so they were naked. A film was made of this hideous cruelty and sent for Hitler and Goebbels to see.

If Hitler had been killed on 20 July 1944 there might have been a negotiated peace, which would have saved Germany from the devastating destruction of the next eight months.

V

THE
UNITED STATES
OF
AMERICA

'No one will wish to hurt me.'

PRESIDENT MCKINLEY

Four presidents of the United States have been assassinated: Abraham Lincoln (1865), James Garfield (1881), William McKinley (1901) and John F. Kennedy (1963). Lincoln was killed by a political opponent; McKinley by an anarchist; Garfield by a lunatic; and Kennedy by a lone gunman whose motive has never been satisfactorily determined.

None of these assassinations promoted a political change, but in Lincoln and Kennedy America lost two outstanding leaders, world figures, who both managed to represent to the world some of the very best ideas, attitudes and actions that make up America.

In addition, four American presidents have been shot at by lunatics: Andrew Jackson in 1835; Theodore Roosevelt when running for a third term in 1912; Gerald Ford, attacked twice by two women in 1975; and Ronald Reagan in 1981.

In 1950 two Puerto Rican nationalists tried to break in and shoot President Harry Truman in Blair House in Washington. They were both shot on the front steps of the building by sentry guards.

When L B Johnson was asked why he accepted Kennedy's invitation to be the Vice-President, which was usually a dead-end job, he had worked out that seven Presidents had died in office for various reasons and therefore he had a 1 in 5 chance of succeeding.

AMERICAN PRESIDENTS

Andrew Jackson
30 January 1835

The President had attended the funeral of a Congressman. As he left the Rotunda of the Capitol in Washington a housepainter, Richard Lawrence, got to within eight feet of him and fired a pistol. Only the cap exploded. He tried again with a second shot and once again only the cap exploded. Jackson, totally unhurt, rushed up to Lawrence and beat him with his cane, shouting, 'Let me alone! Let me alone! I know where he came from.' For the rest of his life he was convinced that Lawrence had been put up to the attack by his Whig opponents. Lawrence however had no political connections: he had been brought by his parents from England and had come to believe that he was Richard III, King of England: he had two English estates, and the President was preventing him getting any money from them. The jury only took five minutes to find him insane, and he died in an asylum in 1861.

Andrew Jackson's escape

Abraham Lincoln
14 April 1865

Abraham Lincoln had made a late entry into American politics when he failed to be nominated as the senator for Illinois in 1858. Two years later he got the Republican nomination for the presidency and won the election, whereupon some of the Southern states decided to leave the union and form a Confederation. Lincoln looked upon this as a rebellion which challenged the very existence of a united American nation, and civil war became inevitable. Robert E. Lee, the general leading the Southern Army, had some early victories, but Lincoln managed to pass the Emancipation Proclamation in September 1862 which abolished slavery in all the Southern states and gave the Northern – Union – Army a political objective. When the Union Army won the Battle of Gettysburg, Lincoln made the most inspiring speech in American history. He appointed Ulysses S. Grant to be the general in command of all the North's forces, and after a bitter war Lee and the Confederate Army of Northern Virginia finally surrendered on 9 April 1865. A grateful nation had re-elected Lincoln in 1864.

On Good Friday, 14 April 1865, Lincoln and his wife Mary went to Ford's Theatre in Washington to see a comedy, *Our American Cousin*. At the last minute Grant and his wife dropped out and their daughter and her fiancé replaced them. There were no special security arrangements, in spite of the fact that Lincoln had asked the War Department to provide a special guard. His only bodyguard was Patrolman John F. Parker, who had been told to stand outside the President's box. First he wandered off to watch the play, and after the interval he left the theatre for a drink in a nearby tavern.

The assassin was a twenty-six-year-old actor, John Wilkes Booth, a rabid supporter of the South. For weeks he had been drinking heavily and declaring that he had a plan to kidnap Lincoln, but neither the police nor the security services had picked up on that. He simply opened the door to the box and fired his one-shot Derringer pistol into Lincoln's head, shouting out, 'Sic semper tyrannis' (So to all tyrants). Booth then jumped on to the stage, declaring, 'The

The unprotected President

South is avenged', rushed out of the theatre, and rode off on his horse. He had a fellow conspirator, David Herold, who had botched an assassination attempt on the Secretary of State, William Seward. An award of $30,000 was announced. Ten days later the two men were cornered in a tobacco shed on a farm in Virginia and ordered to surrender or be burnt out. Herold ran out before it was set on fire; Booth was seen limping, so he was shot as he was pulled out of the fire. His last

The Victim

The Assassin

The hanging of four of the Lincoln conspirators. The one on the left is Mary Surratt.

words were 'Tell Mother I died for my country.'

The Government unearthed a conspiracy of nine people who had tried and failed, and Booth himself had bungled three previous attempts. The conspirators realised their luck had turned when they learnt that the Lincolns were going to the theatre. After a long trial three conspirators were imprisoned for life and four were sentenced to death, including a woman, Mrs Mary Surratt, who owned the house where the conspirators met. She had nothing to do with the plot, and it was expected that she would be pardoned. Not so. On 7 July she and the others were hanged in a prison yard, and the public were allowed to see their dead bodies. As with other famous assassinations the rumour mill was busy with claims that the conspiracy was funded by a much larger group of cotton and gold speculators and radical politicians. Some even said that it was not Booth who was shot.

There were no political consequences of this murder. The great changes that the Civil War was going to create could not be rolled back: they were irreversible. America was firmly on another path. Lincoln was killed at the high point of his career, a victorious leader with a worldwide reputation, a great reformer who had changed the future of his country: his status could not be higher. He did not have to suffer the possibility of another ten years that could not be as good as the previous ten. There was no long twilight to cloud his reputation: he died at the peak of his popularity.

James Garfield
2 July 1881

James Garfield was the first American president to be born in a log cabin. From that humble farming background he advanced by studying Law and by getting into local politics in Ohio. He firmly supported the North in the Civil War, and became a general. In 1880 he unexpectedly won the Republican nomination for the presidential election, and went on to win handsomely. After his first summer as president he decided to leave for a brief holiday. As he entered the Baltimore and Potomac Railway Station in Washington on the morning of 2 July 1881 he was

National Police Gazette 1881

shot twice, in the arm and then in the back, by Charles J. Guiteau. There were no security guards protecting him.

Guiteau, having switched from the Democrats to the Republicans, was convinced that the support he had given Garfield in the election had secured his victory and expected as a reward to be made ambassador to Austria, or perhaps consul in Paris, despite the fact that he spoke no foreign language and had not expressed any interest in those countries. He had made personal requests to both Garfield and the Secretary of State, and been turned down.

At first it seemed that Garfield's wound was not lethal, as he could sit up in bed and eat porridge. The doctors could not find the bullet: they kept on probing with their unwashed hands and unsterilised instruments, which led to blood poisoning. The President lingered on for two and a half months; all America waited for daily reports on his condition, but he died slowly, more the victim of his doctors than his assassin, ending in Elberon, New Jersey, where he had been taken for cooler air, on 19 September.

Daily reports of Garfield's medical condition captivated America, but when he was likely to die from blood poisoning they turned to revenge upon his assassin. This illustration from the National Police Gazette of 1881 captured the spirit of a lynch mob. Guiteau was found guilty but not insane and was hanged a year later.

William McKinley
6 September 1901

'No one will wish to hurt me.'

William McKinley had become the twenty-fifth president of the United States by winning the election in 1896; he then went on to be re-elected in 1900. On 6 September 1901 he was in Buffalo, New York, where he planned to make a major speech on expanding America's trade overseas at a big industrial fair. He was very popular, and could expect a large turnout to cheer and support him. He did not like having his guards around. His personal secretary had tried to get him to cancel the visit to the fair on security grounds, but McKinley answered: 'Why should I? No one will wish to hurt me.'

After his well-received speech the President went on to welcome the delegates. His guards insisted that those who wanted to shake his hand should

"No one will wish to hurt me"

carry nothing, but they did let through a swarthy individual whose right hand was bandaged. As McKinley started to shake the left hand of this man he fired two shots into the President from a gun concealed in his bandages, shouting: 'I've done my duty.' Leon Czolgosz, a twenty-eight-year-old anarchist, was immediately seized; McKinley muttered, 'Be easy with him boys.'

As with Garfield, the doctors could not find the bullet lodged in McKinley's abdomen: the lighting in the room where he was examined was very poor, and there was no surgeon in Buffalo who specialised in stomach surgery. Again doctors poked around with unwashed hands and unsterilised instruments. Gangrene attacked McKinley's pancreas, and eight days later he died. Czolgosz was known to the authorities, but on that day he was clearly not recognised. He was so eccentric that the anarchist newspaper *The Free Society* had warned its readers to have nothing to do with him as he was a dangerous crank. His trial was short, and he died in the electric chair on 29 October.

Following this assassination Congress directed the Secret Service to protect the President of the United States as part of its mandate.

Theodore Roosevelt
14 October 1912

Theodore Roosevelt after two terms as president decided to stand down for Howard Taft. He soon tired of Taft's conservative policies, and split the Republicans by setting up his own party, the Progressive ('Bull Moose') Party, to fight the 1912 election. It got its strange name when Roosevelt replied to a question about his fitness with 'I am as fit as a bull moose'.

After campaigning in Milwaukee on 14 October Roosevelt left a hotel to get into his car to attend an evening rally. A man, John Nepomuk Schrank, stepped right up to him and fired a .38 revolver, hitting him in the chest. One of the crowd stopped the assassin from firing a second shot and Schrank was seized, the crowd shouting, 'Lynch him. Kill him.' Roosevelt said, 'Don't kill him', for his life had been saved by a metal spectacles case and the thick wedge of his fifty-page speech in his pocket. Although he was covered in blood he went on to the meeting and answered questions for over an hour. As an expert on big game hunting he knew that since he was not coughing up blood his lungs had not been hit. He told his supporters: 'I don't know whether you understand that I have just been shot, but it takes more than that to kill a bull moose.' At the hospital the doctors could not find the bullet, so it stayed with him for the rest of his life.

Schrank was clearly mad. He said that after McKinley's assassination in 1901 his ghost had appeared to him, accusing Roosevelt of planning the murder. In 1912 the ghost had reappeared, and urged him: 'Let not a murderer take the Presidential chair. Avenge my death.'

The spectacle case and speech that saved Roosevelt

Franklin Delano Roosevelt
15 February 1933

Franklin Delano Roosevelt was Governor of New York from 1929 to 1933, and it was from that platform that he launched his presidential campaign in 1932, beating Herbert Hoover, who only took six states. On 15 February 1933, as president elect, he was returning from a twelve-day fishing holiday on Vincent Astor's yacht which came to port in Miami, Florida. Roosevelt decided to stop in a nearby park and deliver a short speech. FDR noticed that the Mayor of Chicago, Anton Cermak, was in the crowd and beckoned him to the front. This was to be fatal for Cermak. Giuseppe Zangara, standing about twenty-five feet away, fired five shots from a .32 calibre revolver which he had purchased for $8. One of the shots entered Cermak's lung. Roosevelt, who was not hit, cradled the Mayor on his way to hospital, where he lingered for three weeks before he died.

There is no doubt that Roosevelt was not the target. Zangara would not have known that Roosevelt was going to be in Miami, and had already decided to

FDR, with Mayor Cermak on his right

kill the Mayor. The question arose who paid for the bullet. Cermak was deeply involved in dealing with Al Capone in Chicago, and he had established links with a rival Mafia family. Zangara's dying words in the electric chair were 'Lousy capitalists'.

Harry S. Truman
1 November 1950

In this attempt two smartly dressed Puerto Ricans, Oscar Collazo and Griselio Torresola, tried to break into Blair House, where President Truman was living while the White House was being restored. Collazo led the attack, wounding one of the presidential guards, Donald Birdzell, but the exchange of fire alerted other guards; they turned on the second assassin, who had shot and killed a sentry guard. Torresola was killed by a bullet to his head, and Birdzell, although wounded, managed to shoot Collazo. Collazo recovered from his wound and was sentenced to death, but President Truman commuted his sentence to life imprisonment.

Collazo, shot at the foot of Blair House steps

This would-be assassination clearly had a political motive, the independence of Puerto Rico. In his defence Collazo stated: 'I didn't come here to plead for my life. I came here to plead for the cause of liberty of my people.'

For two assassins to try to kill the President in his house was an absurd, impossible and insane act, for there were at least twenty security guards at various points.

John F. Kennedy
22 November 1963

More has been written on this assassination than any other, and probably more than all the others put together. The one indisputable fact is that the President was killed by two bullets fired at 12:30pm on 22 November 1963 while he was being driven through Dallas in an open-topped car, sitting next to his wife and behind the Governor of Texas, John B. Connolly, and his wife. Kennedy was shot by Lee Harvey Oswald, who worked for the Texas School Book Depository.

A minute before

He had fired possibly three bullets from a sixth-floor window.

Oswald left his rifle in the Depository but he kept a revolver, and when stopped by a policeman, John Tippit, he killed him with four bullets. He then fled to hide in a movie house and when he was flushed out he tried to fire again, but this time his pistol misfired. Oswald denied killing either the President or Tippit, but several witnesses saw him kill Tippit, and his palm print was found on the rifle he left behind.

Two days after Oswald's arrest when he was being transferred to the County Jail he was shot and killed by Jack Ruby, a nightclub owner. That murder was seen on television.

Then the rumours began. One that did not run was that the Dallas Police were purposefully slack in protecting Oswald, hoping to conceal the fact that they had been involved in the assassination or its cover up. What was grist to this mill was the discovery of a home movie camera used by Abraham Zapruder which opened up the possibility of a second gunman standing on a grassy knoll, which gave more fuel to the rumour that Oswald was not acting alone. That

A minute after

The assassin Lee Harvey Oswald assassinated by Jack Ruby

seemed to be supported by Connolly's assertion that he had been hit by a second bullet. Could a possible accomplice have come from the KGB? Oswald had been to Russia: there he had tried to give up American citizenship, married a Russian, and trained to be an expert rifleman. After two years the Russians slung him out and he returned to America, where he dallied with the Communist Party and the Socialist Workers Party. Could he have been a Soviet spy?

A Select Committee on Assassinations identified acoustic evidence of further shots, and also unearthed Oswald's and Jack Ruby's involvement in Mafia crime. A further committee of ballistic experts rubbished the acoustic evidence. Then there were many books on a variety of conspiracies: one even claimed that Oswald had a personal vendetta against Connolly, who was the real target; another argued that Lyndon B. Johnson, the Vice-President, had planned the assassination to become president. The involvement of the Mafia was a strong runner, in spite of denials from various Mafia leaders who said it was not their policy to kill police officers, FBI agents or high public officials.

Under the 1992 Kennedy Assassination Records Act, promoted by the CIA, certain files could not be disclosed until October 2017. President Trump was only too delighted to release them, because he believed there was a conspiracy and had actually hinted that the father of Ted Cruz, one of his Republican rivals, was involved in it. The relevant papers revealed that seven weeks before the assassination Oswald had gone to Mexico, where in the Soviet Embassy he met Valery Vladimirovich Kostikov, a KGB officer in Department 13 – a unit 'responsible for sabotage and assassination'. This hinted at the possibility of the KGB being involved in Kennedy's assassination, but that is most unlikely. It also questioned the CIA's failure to keep surveillance on Oswald.

In my view the original findings of the Warren Commission got at the truth. Only a trained sniper could hit a moving target several hundred yards away, and Kennedy was hit first in his back and then in his head. Moreover, when Oswald left his apartment after breakfast that morning he left his wedding ring in a cup on the dresser and $170 in a wallet in a drawer. He was not expecting to come back. His marriage had descended to violence and mutual contempt, and he was ashamed of his failure to kill General Walker, missing him when he tried to shoot him through a window in his house. He wanted to prove to the world that he was not a failure.

Kennedy's death was a worldwide tragedy. He was a president who represented the very best of America, carrying all the country's hopes for a better world. Handsome and charismatic, Kennedy and his beautiful wife were the closest America came to having a royal family. As the leader of the free world he had been tested to the limit in the Cuban crisis a year earlier, taking America to the very brink of a world war in facing down Khrushchev. The world was safe in his hands, and he had a way of cutting through to ordinary people, as in his famous speech in Berlin when he declared 'Ich bin ein Berliner' – 'I am a Berliner, one of you.' The writer John Updike commented on the assassination, 'God might have withdrawn his blessing from America.'

Many people remember exactly what they were doing when they heard of Kennedy's death. The news reached Europe in the early evening. Mary and I were sitting in the Royal Festival Hall for a performance of Benjamin Britten's opera Gloriana, where E. M. Forster was to be present. We had not heard the news before it started, but we were surprised that there were so many empty seats and that the audience was talking in very hushed tones. We only learnt of Kennedy's death from the car radio on the way home.

If Kennedy had not been assassinated would the history of the world be different?

Would he have brought the war in Vietnam to an earlier end than his successor? Lyndon B. Johnson, sworn in on the day of the assassination, intensified America's support for South Vietnam, which was to lead to over 500,000 American soldiers fighting and many dying there, and would result in America's humiliating defeat. Could JFK have avoided that?

In 1945 Ho Chi Minh started what was a peasants' revolt against France's colonial control of Indochina, which consisted of Vietnam, Laos and Cambodia. Their neighbours were Thailand, Malaysia and Singapore – the latter two being part of the British Empire. Ho Chi Minh had the support of Russia and Communist China, while France was supported by the USA, on the grounds of the Domino Theory that if one country fell to the Communists all the others would fall.

By 1954 the USA was spending $1 billion a year in Vietnam, and had parachuted heavy weapons and many paratroopers into the large military base which the French were building in North Vietnam at Dien Bien Phu. Ho Chi Minh's brilliant commander-in-chief, General Giap, laid siege to that base and after four months of heavy and fierce fighting the French had to surrender.

Six years later, when JFK was president, South Vietnam had become the battlefield between Communism and the Free World. America by helping South Vietnam was protecting other countries in South East Asia. Not surprisingly,

Lee Kwan Yew, President of Singapore, made his view very clear to the British Government: 'You must go to Vietnam and help hold my frontline.'

In 1960 there were 750 military advisers in Vietnam, but by 1963 JFK had sent 22,000 Americans – soldiers, sailors, airmen, technicians and agriculturalists – to help the Vietnamese Army repel the attacks that the Vietcong were making on villages in the South. The speech that Kennedy was going to make in Dallas on the day he was assassinated included these words: 'We in this country, in this generation, are the watchmen on the walls of freedom . . . our assistance to . . . nations can be painful, risky and costly . . . As true in South East Asia today. But we do not weary of the task.'

JFK was preoccupied with the presidential election due a year later and he was not prepared to be the president who let South Vietnam be absorbed into the Communist fold, however badly the country was governed – and it was being governed very badly.

Kennedy's team of advisers, whom Lyndon Johnson was to inherit, were Robert McNamara, Secretary of State for Defence; McGeorge Bundy, National Security Adviser; Dean Rusk, Secretary of State; and Walt Rostow, Chairman of the Policy Planning Council. They were strong advocates for stepping up America's support in Vietnam. McNamara and Rostow, supported by the Rand Corporation, were convinced that North Vietnam could be bombed into submission by the overwhelming military might of America.

Kennedy was also embroiled in the internal politics of Vietnam. Nineteen days before his own assassination, the President of South Vietnam, Ngo Dinh Diem, was assassinated by a group of generals. The Americans knew about the coup: it was strongly advocated by the American Ambassador to Vietnam, Henry Cabot Lodge Jr. He kept Kennedy informed, as he was the only person who could have stopped the coup, but he did not. By acquiescing, he was locking in America to improve the government of South Vietnam – a long term measure that became an engulfing mire and proved to be impossible.

In the year between Kennedy's assassination in 1963 and the 1964 presidential election the Vietcong expanded the area it had 'liberated' in the South and China

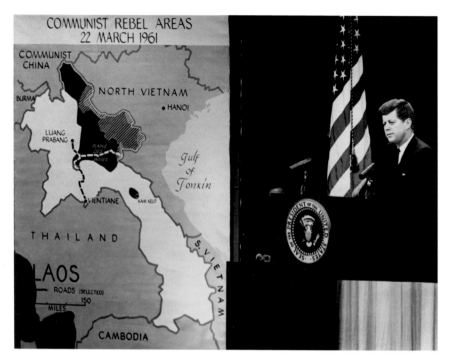

"We do not weary of the task", President Kennedy

stepped up its support with more weapons. In those circumstances Kennedy could not have disengaged America. America's credibility was at stake, and letting Hanoi take over Saigon would have been a humiliating defeat for the most powerful country in the world.

So the conclusion I have reached is that the policy of Kennedy, remarkable as he was and undoubtedly a great national leader, would not have differed fundamentally from that which LBJ implemented.

Robert Kennedy, a possible president
5 June 1968

On 5 June 1968 Robert Kennedy won the California presidential primary, defeating Senator Eugene McCarthy, and became a real contender for the Democratic candidacy in the presidential election later that year. He made a victory speech in his HQ in the Ambassador Hotel in Los Angeles, then to make it easier for him to get out, avoiding the massed ranks of his supporters, he was led just after midnight through a service pantry to leave by the back door. A twenty-four-year-old Palestinian immigrant, Sirhan Sirhan, was there, carrying a Kennedy poster that concealed his pistol. He fired several shots, two hitting Kennedy in his armpit which were not fatal, but the third entered Kennedy's head above his right eye and that killed him. Sirhan shouted out: 'Kennedy you son of a bitch!' He was quickly overpowered. At that time

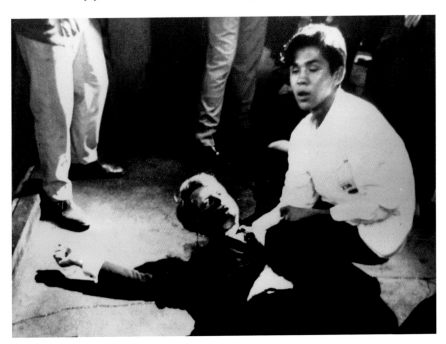

The death of the brother

although presidents had full security, candidates had none.

The rumours soon started: there were over eight shots and someone else might have been involved, but these could have been ricochets. One of Kennedy's personal guards, Thomas Cesar, was momentarily a suspect, but his revolver was a .38 and none of that type of bullet was recovered. Again, one of Kennedy's supporters had seen two men and a woman wearing a polka dot dress go into the hotel; when he saw them come out the woman said, 'We shot him.' Answering his question she said, 'We shot Kennedy'. The woman was traced – Cathy Fulmer – and she was found dead in a hotel room after Sirhan had been convicted. Then there were rumours that the Mafia had planned to kill Kennedy because he had been very hard on them as Attorney General and would be even harder if he became president. Sirhan had once worked as a groom at the Santa Anita Racetrack which was controlled by the local Mafia boss, Mickey Cohen, but at the time of the assassination Cohen was in prison, semi-paralysed.

Everything was soon known about Sirhan. His library card revealed that he had taken out a lot of books on the Middle East. He was known for his extreme hatred of Jews and Israel, and what drove him to hate Kennedy was a speech Kennedy had made supporting the despatch of more bomber planes to Israel. Sirhan had written in his diary on 19 May: 'RFK must die. RFK must be killed. Robert F. Kennedy must be assassinated.' Sirhan was condemned to death, but Robert's brother Edward Kennedy pleaded for this to be commuted to a life sentence and he is still in jail.

Later, in a television interview when David Frost was allowed to speak to Sirhan in prison, he said that if Kennedy had left by the front door he would never have got close enough to kill him.

If Robert Kennedy had become the presidential candidate instead of Hubert Humphry, he would have fought Richard Nixon. Who knows what might have happened?

Gerald Ford
5 September and 22 September 1975

On 5 September 1975 Lynette 'Squeaky' Fromme, a twenty-six-year-old member of the Manson Family commune, centred on the murderer Charles Manson, got within two feet of President Ford at a conference in Sacramento (where Manson was in jail). She levelled her gun to shoot him in the chest, but it was knocked from her hand by an alert guard and never went off. Fromme, although not insane, was deranged through her devotion to the cult of Manson.

Three weeks later, on 22 September, another mentally disturbed woman, Sara Jane Moore, who had worked for a time as a spy for the FBI and who believed that she was a target for assassination by the Government, tried to shoot the President. From more than thirty feet away she pointed her .38 calibre pistol at Ford, but a former marine in the crowd grabbed her arms and the bullet missed. She apparently wanted to compensate for her sense of rejection by the FBI by committing a dramatic political act. President Ford was very lucky.

He escaped twice

Only just saved

Ronald Reagan
30 March 1981

As Ronald Reagan was leaving the Hilton Hotel in Washington on 30 March 1981 Joseph Hinckley fired several shots from a .22 calibre pistol. One bullet entered under the President's left armpit, pierced his chest, and ploughed on into the left lower lobe of his lungs. Three of the President's security guards were also hit. The President was bundled into his car; one of the guards lay across him to protect him on the journey to the hospital, for initially the President did not realise he had been shot. Hinckley had also dogged President Carter in 1980, but alert police had confiscated his weapons at an airport. It is extraordinary that after that he was not subjected to security surveillance.

The reason why Hinckley attempted the assassination was explained in a letter he had written to the movie star Jodie Foster and posted to her only a couple of hours before he shot Reagan: he was shooting the President for her sake, because he wanted to impress her with his love and his wish to live with her for the rest of his life. To the dismay of many Americans, Hinckley's jury found him not guilty but insane. He was sent to a psychiatric hospital, and released in 2016.

Reagan was quite seriously wounded, but his ability to joke about the incident, even while undergoing medical care, endeared him to the nation and contributed to a dramatic recovery in his approval rating.

OTHER IMPORTANT AMERICAN ASSASSINATIONS

Martin Luther King
4 April 1968

Martin Luther King was born in Atlanta, Georgia, to a very religious family. In the sight of God black people were equal to white, but not in the eyes of most Americans living in the Southern states. After Lincoln had abolished slavery in 1865 the Southern whites continued to believe that blacks were inferior, so it was right to deny them the vote and the right to marry whites; of black children only 0.1 per cent attended a mixed-race school.

After studying at a theological seminary in Pennsylvania and Boston University, in 1954 King became the pastor of a Baptist church in Montgomery, Alabama. It was in that town a year later that Rosa Parks, a black seamstress, was arrested for sitting in the part of a bus reserved for whites. King became a leader of the campaign to attack segregation that lasted for more than a year. There was no violence from his side, but bombs were thrown at his house. In 1956 the Supreme Court decided that Alabama's segregation of bus seats was unconstitutional.

This campaign made King a national figure and showed that a pastor could become the leading protagonist in the fight for equal civil rights. Like Gandhi, whom he admired, he preached that protest should be non-violent. It was his opponents, like the Ku Klux Klan, who resorted to violence and murder.

After Kennedy's presidential victory in 1960 King joined student protestors sitting in a segregated restaurant, and this developed into a national protest. King was arrested and jailed, but released by Robert Kennedy, the Attorney General. He became a well-known figure not just in America but across the world.

On 28 August 1963 King, with other civil rights groups, organised a massive march to Washington to persuade President Kennedy that legislation was needed to end discrimination. Initially King was apprehensive because he did not think enough would turn up, but over 250,000 gathered, and in front of the Lincoln Memorial King made his famous speech, 'I have a dream': 'I have a dream that my four little children will one day live in a nation where they will not be judged by the color of their skin but by the content of their character.'

By this time King had earned the undying hostility of J. Edgar Hoover, the head of the FBI, who described him as 'the most dangerous and effective negro

Hero of the rally

King's friends pointing at the window where the shot was fired

leader'. Hoover was convinced that King was a Communist, and subjected him to intense surveillance over many years. King's phones were tapped: Hoover discovered that he had a number of extramarital affairs and told King's wife about them, but the news didn't become public until 2019.

On 4 April 1968 King went to Memphis, Tennessee, to support a strike by the city's sanitation workers over their working practices compared to those of white workers. He stepped out of his room to have a cigarette on the balcony. It was a huge stroke of misfortune, for at that very moment the assassin had trained his rifle on that balcony, and a bullet severed King's spinal cord. His assassin was a white man, James Earl Ray, a habitual criminal. A rumour arose that there had been a conspiracy and that large sums had been offered for King's death, but the House Select Committee on Assassinations found no convincing evidence. Later a jury in 1999 ruled out that there had been a conspiracy.

Later in police custody James Earl Ray claimed he was under the control of a mysterious character called Raoul. He was in fact a loner, who had worked out that in order to get a direct sight of King's balcony he had to stand with the rifle in his hands in the bathtub of the communal bathroom in the hotel where he was staying. When he was finally arrested, he had in his possession only a Liberty Chief .38 revolver, a pamphlet entitled *How to Hypnotise*, two bars of soap, a birth certificate bearing the name Raymond George Sneyd, two paperback novels, a brown woollen suit, and a book entitled *Psycho-Cybernetics*. He died in prison thirty years later.

If Ray and others had hoped that by killing King they would halt the Civil Rights movement they were utterly wrong. King died at the peak of his popularity, and his assassination made him a martyr. His 'I have a dream' speech became an inspiration for all those who fight for equal rights.

In 2019 various documents were released, including some covering the electronic surveillance of King by the FBI. These papers resulted in a long article by David Garrow, a Pulitzer Prize-winning journalist, which was turned down by the *Guardian* and the *Washington Post* and eventually printed by the respected British monthly magazine *Standpoint* on 30 May. It revealed that Martin Luther King was a serial womaniser, who spent a good deal of his time arranging his affairs with over forty-seven women. On one occasion in a Washington hotel he had watched a colleague rape a woman and laughingly encouraged him. He had been present at other orgies, and was a binge-drinker. Garrow concluded that this evidence – and more is expected to be released in 2027 – will lead to 'a profoundly painful historical reckoning', though some have cast doubt on the FBI tapes. This was the assassination of Martin Luther King's reputation, but it does not diminish his civil rights achievements.

Osama bin Laden
2011

Osama bin Laden left college in Saudi Arabia in 1979 when he was twenty-two years old to go to Pakistan to help the Mujahedeen fight against the Soviet forces occupying Afghanistan. Accepting Allah's words as his authority to establish Sharia (Islamic law), he devoted his life to promoting Islam across the world and protecting it when it was threatened. All of his opponents – first the Soviets, then the Americans, and always the Jews – had to be driven out and killed. He was to become the most famous terrorist in the world, asserting the moral use of violence.

Osama bin Laden

In 1987 he led two dozen Arab fighters across the border into Afghanistan and established a compound at al-Masala which became a training centre for terrorists and suicide bombers. The Russians failed to destroy it. In 1988 he was the founder and spiritual leader of al-Qaeda ('the Base'), a terrorist organisation that he backed with his considerable fortune of £20 million inherited from his father. This allowed him to recruit teams of experts to create a communications system to plan and implement attacks on American embassies. In 1998 he told an American television journalist: 'I am declaring war on the United States. I am going to attack your country.' America took little heed of a crackpot Arab, since its President Bill Clinton had other things on his mind (including a charge of sexual impropriety with a White House intern, Monica Lewinsky). Bin Laden had one advantage: 'We love death, the US love life, that is the big difference between us.'

Bin Laden was determined to strike at the Twin Towers of the World Trade

Center in New York, the symbols of American wealth and power. Al-Qaeda recruited and trained all the suicide bombers who on 11 September 2001 flew the first plane into one tower and twenty minutes later the second into the other tower, and later a third into the Pentagon in Washington. He did not care that thousands of innocent civilians were killed: 'We will kill civilian infidels in exchange for those of our children they kill.' The president by then was George W. Bush. He vowed to hunt bin Laden down, but his interest flagged after he launched the war in Iraq in 2003. Little attention was giving to finding where bin Laden was living, and he dropped out of the public's attention.

When Obama became president things changed. In 2009, just four months into his presidency, he called together Leon Panetta, the new CIA Director, Mike Leiter, Director of the National Counter-Terrorism Center, his deputy Tom Donilon, and his Chief of Staff. Obama told them: 'Here's the deal. I want the hunt for Osama bin Laden . . . to come to the front line. I worry that the trail has gone cold. This has to be our first priority . . . you need to insure that we have expended every effort to take down the top leadership of al-Qaeda.' To reinforce this he asked for a report each month, which meant they all had to focus on the task, as none would want to report no action.

These agencies, with renewed energy and using powerful computers, collated a huge amount of information from emails, phones, spies on the ground, plane tickets, invoices, employment records, casual meetings and unusual behaviour. They came to focus upon a compound in a small town in the cooler hills 70 miles north of Islamabad called Abbottabad, which was a quiet resort named after its founder, Major James Abbott, an officer of the British Raj. The recently built compound was surrounded by an 18-foot wall topped with barbed wire. Inside there were some outbuildings and a three-storey house which had very few windows, all of which had been coated with a material that stopped anyone from seeing in. Four adult males, five women and twenty children lived in it, as well as a tall man who exercised by walking around the building, but it was not possible for an aerial camera to see his face. Very few people came and went, and the children were only let out to visit a doctor. The Americans did not fly drones

Bin Laden's house in Abbottabad

over the compound, since that could alert the inhabitants that they were under observation and they might leave. This group of people had been living there for six years.

By March 2011 it was agreed that the compound held 'a high value target', but no one was 100 per cent certain that it was bin Laden. Obama accepted that there were two courses of action. First was a bombing raid to destroy the building and kill all the occupants. This was an action without any risk to American soldiers, but the disadvantage was that you could never be sure that it was bin Laden who had been killed, and Obama would not want to be the president who ordered the killing of twenty children. The second course was a raid involving four helicopters and twenty-four soldiers, including eight highly trained special services officers known as Navy Seals. They would have to fly from Afghanistan, some 150 miles, and escape detection by the Pakistan Air Force. Two of the helicopters would land in the compound, and within half an hour the eight Seals

The Committee of Assassins

would either kill or arrest bin Laden and return with no loss of American lives. In April this plan was tested twice by dummy attacks on buildings that had been specially built to resemble the compound. It was agreed that the mission would take place in the early days of May when there would be no moon. The elaborate preparation meant that there were scores of people who knew about the raid, and there was a real danger that somehow it would leak, so it had to be implemented or abandoned. Obama also wanted to keep open the option of a missile attack that would destroy the tall man.

On 28 April eleven people met in the Situation Room in the White House – the President; the Vice-President, Joe Biden; the Defense Secretary, Robert Gates; the Secretary of State, Hillary Clinton; the Chairman of the Joint Chiefs of Staff, Admiral Muller; Vice-Chairman General Cartwright; John Brennan; Tom Donilon; Director of National Intelligence James Clapper; the CIA Director Leon Panetta; and his deputy, Michael Morel. This was the jury that had to recommend to the President what he should do. There were three options:

approve a raid, approve a missile strike, or do nothing. Everyone had to give their opinion. Nine approved the raid; the two dissenters were Joe Biden ('We have to do more things to see if he is there') and Robert Gates (who preferred the missile attack). Obama said he would sleep on it and inform them of his decision the following morning.

Overnight the two deputies to Robert Gates persuaded him to support the raid, but Joe Biden did not change his view. At 8am the following morning Obama told Donilon and his Chief of Staff: 'It's go – we're going to do the raid. Prepare the directives.' The group of assassins met again, and were able to watch the raid because high over Abbottabad a stealth drone was flying with a high-power lens to provide live video feed.

The assassins saw the helicopters land (one struck the compound wall and became inoperative), and they watched the Seals enter on the ground floor and shoot four people, one of whom was a son of bin Laden, Khalid. They shot on sight, as they feared that some of the guards would be strapped into explosive vests.

The Seals moved up to the third floor, where they found bin Laden. He was protected by his latest wife, Amal, but they shot him in his chest and in his eye. None of the women, three of whom were bin Laden's wives, or the four children was hit. It was the children who told the Seals that the man who had been shot was their father, Osama bin Laden. His body was zipped into a nylon bag and carried downstairs where a medic in the group unzipped the bag, took samples of blood, and inserted needles to remove bone marrow for DNA testing. After the wrecked helicopter was burnt, all the Seals were returned to safety in the two helicopters that had landed outside the compound. The whole operation took just thirty minutes.

Bin Laden's body was offered to Saudi Arabia, which refused to take it, so he was buried at sea.

This was a revenge assassination. Bin Laden's capacity to get al-Qaeda to plan another major terrorist event had reduced significantly, as there was no longer a team around him to respond to his ideas. After the invasion of Iraq he

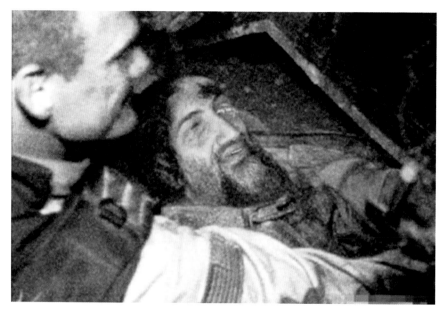

The end of the leading terrorist

felt he was being upstaged by Abu Bakr al-Baghdadi, the leader of the Islamic State, and in the Yemen it was Anwar al-Awlaki who planned terrorist attacks.

In February 2012 the Pakistan authorities demolished the compound. No shrine.

In 2019 the American Government offered a bounty of $1 million for any information about or the arrest of Hamza bin Laden, the son of Osama, looked upon as the crown prince of the al-Qaeda terrorist group. In an interview he said: 'If you think your sinful crime that you committed in Abbottabad has passed without punishment, then you are wrong.' He is thought to be living in the Afghanistan/Pakistan border area, planning an attack upon America. Hamza, like the son of Duncan in Macbeth, would not let the murder of his father go unavenged. However, in August 2019 American officials announced that Hamza bin Laden had been killed, but without revealing the details. 9/11 was a poisoned chalice for the bin Laden family.

Baitullah Mehsud
5 August 2009

Baitullah Mehsud was a leading militant in Waziristan, Pakistan. From 2004 to 2009 he was Governor of the Mehsud area (his family region), from where he organised many attacks; he was responsible for 85 per cent of suicide bombings and for the bomb outrage at Rawalpindi in 2007. In that year he formed a new party, Tehrik-i-Taliban Pakistan (TTP), from five militant groups, and at one time he commanded 5,000 fighters who attacked Pakistan's army, government and officials. In the spring of 2009 he struck at the heart of government by attacking a police training facility in Lahore because they cooperated with the United States on drone strikes. Mehsud also made the extraordinary claim that a shooting by a sole deranged Vietnamese man in Binghamton, New York, on 13 April 2009, where thirteen Americans were killed, was his responsibility: 'They were my men.' This was a fantasy, but America had had enough.

Baitullah and a bodyguard

It was rumoured that Mehsud had planned the assassination of Benazir Bhutto on 27 December 2007. He denied the CIA claim that he had, with the help of al-Qaeda, carried out this murder, but George W. Bush placed his name on a 'classified list of militant leaders whom the CIA and American commandos were authorised to capture or kill'.

In June 2009 the Pakistan Government offered a reward of 50,000,000 rupees for any information as to his whereabouts, and that was alongside a bounty offered by the United States of $5,000,000. On 5 August 2009, while he was staying with his second wife at his father-in-law's in Zangar, South Waziristan, he was hit by a US drone. The CIA Director Leon Panetta confirmed that he had been seen on the roof of the house, identified by his distinctive hat. His followers at first denied that he had been killed, but President Obama on 20 August confirmed in a radio address that 'we took out Mehsud'.

The CIA and Foreign Regimes

In promoting American and democratic interests across the world, the CIA did not consider organising assassination attempts apart from the period 1960–76 after Fidel Castro, a committed Communist, had won power in Cuba. A meeting of the National Security Council on 10 March 1960 suggested that the assassination of Fidel, his brother Raúl, and Che Guevara should at least be theoretically considered, and President

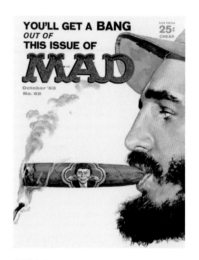

Eisenhower signed off a programme of covert action against the Castro regime called Operation Mongoose – presumably because a mongoose can kill a dangerous snake. A general was appointed to lead the project. After John F. Kennedy became President in January 1961 the general reported directly to Robert Kennedy, the Attorney General.

Plans were put in hand for an attack on Cuba's economy, an attack on key utility plants, a possible invasion, a media war, and an attempt to stir up opposition to Castro

A CIA dream

inside Cuba, but all his real opponents had fled to Florida. The CIA began to plan the assassination of Fidel and Raúl Castro and Che Guevara. Castro's intelligence chief, Fabian Escalante, counted 634 assassination attempts, many of them quite ludicrous.

The CIA dismissed the idea of assassination by gunfire, as an assassin could not get near enough to Fidel and afterwards could not escape. So they considered poisoned cigars, a liquid poison that would kill within three days, and a ballpoint pen with a secret poisoned hypodermic needle.

As Castro was a keen diver they planned to create a spectacular seashell submerged in an area where he often skin-dived: 'the seashell would be loaded with explosives to blow apart when the shell was lifted'. After investigation it was determined that there was no shell in the Caribbean area large enough to hold sufficient explosive. A similar plot aimed to get Castro to wear a contaminated skin-diving suit. The CIA plan was to dust the inside of the wetsuit with a fungus producing 'Madeira foot', a disabling skin disease, and also to put tuberculosis bacilli in the breathing apparatus.

As the CIA did not have any agents in Cuba capable of planning and executing an assassination, they asked the reclusive Howard Hughes to assemble a team from the Mafia, which included Rosselli, a former lieutenant of Al Capone, and Giancana, a Sicilian mobster who ran the Chicago Mafia. The Mafia took the CIA to the cleaners: no weapons or bombs were sent to Cuba and the boats with hitmen never landed, although Rosselli had been given $150,000 to assassinate Castro. In 1975 Operation Mongoose was cancelled and a Senate Committee was set up to examine government assassinations. This revealed that there had been eight attempts. Strangely enough, both Rosselli and Giancana were assassinated just before they could testify to the Committee. Who paid for the bullets? The CIA or the Mafia?

During the period 1960–76 the CIA did consider other targets apart from Castro. In November 1975 a Senate Select Committee on Intelligence Activities published a document revealing that officials had ordered the assassination of Patrice Lumumba in Zaire and had been involved in assassination plans against three other leaders – Rafael Trujillo of the Dominican Republic, Ngo Dinh Diem of South Vietnam, and General René Schneider of Chile. Four of these were killed, but not by American plans.

Allen Dulles, then Director of the CIA, in August 1960 sent a cable to its head in Zaire about Lumumba, saying: 'removal must be our urgent and prime objective . . . and should be a high priority'. But before any American could act, the politics of Zaire were transformed by the army leader, Mobutu, seizing power. In the civil war Lumumba was captured; two months later he was handed over to the breakaway province of Katanga, and was not heard of again.

President Kennedy was involved in one of the assassinations – Ngo Dinh Diem, the President of South Vietnam, in 1963. Following the withdrawal of France from French Indochina, Vietnam had become the battleground between the North, led by the Communist Ho Chi Minh, supported by Russia and China, and the South, supported by America. With its unstable and incompetent government South Vietnam would have been overrun, but as this was the major conflict in the Cold War with Russia America could not simply abandon it to its fate.

In August 1963 the new American Ambassador to South Vietnam, Henry Cabot Lodge Jr, decided very soon that Diem was incapable of running the country, and a coup led by the army should take place. On 23 August he asked Washington whether it would support a coup. Averell Harriman's reply was that if Diem did not introduce reforms and sack his brother, 'We are prepared to accept the obvious implication that we can no longer support Diem. You may tell appropriate military commanders that we will give them direct support in any period of breakdown.' When JFK saw this telegram, ironically just nineteen days before his own assassination, he decided not to stop it. It was left to Lodge to tell General Duong Van Minh, the leader of the generals, that if there was a coup America would not be involved.

On 1 November Diem asked Lodge for American support, but was only offered safe conduct out of the country. The plotters launched an attack on the presidential palace, but Diem and his brother had slipped out and taken refuge in a Catholic church. On 3 November Diem told Minh that he and his brother would resign unconditionally, and an armoured carrier was sent to collect them from the church. It stopped at a railroad crossing where both were shot. General Minh announced to the public that Diem had committed suicide.

Lodge summoned the generals to his embassy. He described the assassination as 'a remarkable performance in all respects', and cabled Washington: 'the prospects now are a shorter war'. How wrong he was. Ho-Chi Minh's crisper comment from North Vietnam was: 'I can scarcely believe the Americans would be so stupid.' The junta of South Vietnamese generals had no experience of how to run the country, and General Minh had to stand down after four months. It was generally believed that America was behind the assassination, or at the very least did nothing to stop it. It did mean that America was locked into saving South Vietnam as a bulwark against Communism – another poisoned chalice.

The Assassin's Friend – Ambassador Henry Cabot Lodge Jr. (left). The Victim – President Ngo Dinh Diem (right).

One of the KGB's successes in the 1970s was to persuade Indira Gandhi, Prime Minister of India, to believe that the CIA had been responsible for the fall of the Marxist Government in Chile and the death of its leader, Salvador Allende. In March 1973 she told Castro: 'What they [the CIA] have done to Allende they want to do to me also. There are people here, connected with the same foreign forces that acted in Chile, who would like to eliminate me.' She went on to say, 'When I am murdered they will say I arranged it myself.' There has been a great debate about whether Allende was murdered by Pinochet's followers or turned the gun upon himself. It is now generally agreed that Allende did commit suicide, as his doctor had witnessed it. Tragically the real threat to Indira Gandhi came not from the CIA but from her own Sikh bodyguards.

In 1976 President Gerald Ford signed an Executive Order outlawing political assassination.

VI

THE
INDIAN
SUBCONTINENT
&
SRI LANKA

'His murder shows how dangerous it is to be good.'

GEORGE BERNARD SHAW ON GANDHI

INDIA AND PAKISTAN

Mahatma Gandhi
30 January 1948

Mohandas 'Mahatma' Gandhi was one of the most significant figures in the twentieth century, a spiritual and political leader, immediately recognisable and remembered as the key figure in the fight for Indian independence. His unique campaigns were a commitment to non-violent civil disobedience which proved to be very difficult for the Imperial government of Britain.

At eighteen Gandhi left his wife and first child to travel to London to study Law at the Inner Temple. At the age of twenty-two he went with his family to South Africa, where he stayed for twenty-one years working as a lawyer, fighting against colour prejudice and developing the concept of non-violence. Gandhi returned to India in 1915 and encouraged Indians to serve in the British Army, as there was a British promise to help Swaraj (self-government) for Indians after the end of the war. Only minor reforms were introduced. Gandhi developed his campaign of civil disobedience, and Britain's response to make that a criminal offence set the stage for a long struggle.

Gandhi stopped wearing European clothes in favour of a cotton loincloth, leading to Churchill calling him 'a half-naked Fakir'. He became a vegetarian, virtually rejected medical science, and supported the simple and traditional ways of Indian life, like spinning and weaving. The spinning wheel became his trademark.

The loin-cloth winner with the Governor General, Lord Mountbatten

In 1921 he became the leader of the Indian National Congress, which he transformed into the major political organisation with branches in states and districts, its network touching every part of India. In 1922 he was arrested and charged with running a campaign to spread disaffection and to disrupt the government and administration of the country. His plea was: 'The law itself in this country has been used to serve the foreign exploiter . . . Non-violence is the first article of my faith.' The judge did not agree, deciding that what Gandhi was doing was bound to lead to violence, and sentenced him to six years. Over his life he spent more than two thousand days in various Indian prisons. His non-violent campaigns included organised demonstrations, marches, strikes, and press articles. One particular weapon which the British could not counter was his fasts: these led several governor generals to make concessions.

In 1942 Gandhi made a speech in Bombay calling for Britain to quit India, preferably within two years. He was imprisoned again. On his release in 1944 he was alarmed to discover that the Muslims, led by Jinnah, wanted India to be divided into two countries: Muslim Pakistan and Hindu India. Gandhi believed passionately that India should remain one country, with Muslims and Hindus living peacefully side by side. However the political reality was that this division was bound to happen (it was to lead to 10 million Hindus and Muslims migrating across the borders, and over 500,000 being slaughtered). India became independent on 15 August 1947. Gandhi continued to preach for peaceful coexistence, and Mountbatten, the Governor General, asked him to visit Calcutta, the capital of Bengal – a powder-keg. In his late seventies Gandhi walked from village to village threatened with communal strife, from Bengal to Bihar, and extracted promises from the locals that they would not kill each other. He started a fast on 1 September 1947, saying he would fast to his death if he did not have written pledges from the Hindus and Muslims to forego violence. He received that pledge fifteen days later. Mountbatten said he had 55,000 soldiers in the Punjab where there was still large-scale rioting, but in Calcutta just one man had stopped it.

Gandhi did the same by visiting Delhi. There, however, there was a group of passionate and frustrated Hindus known as the Rashtriya Sevak Sangh (RSS) who wanted to precipitate a civil war which they believed they could win and then rule the whole subcontinent. The leader of the RSS was Vinayak Savarkar, a Right-wing Hindu extremist. He published a newspaper edited by Nathuram Godse and Narayan Apte, and these two decided to kill Gandhi, whom they looked upon as a traitor to Hinduism. Their attempt with a bomb on 20 January 1948 failed. Gandhi's comment was: 'Rama is my protector. If he wants to end my life no one can save me.' At his prayer meetings he refused to allow his followers to be searched. On 30 January 1948, in his seventy-eighth year, as he was going to hold a prayer meeting in Delhi, Godse mingled with the crowd, stepped forward, and shot Gandhi in his chest at point blank range. Gandhi gasped, 'He Rama' (Oh God), and before he died he gave a sign of forgiveness to his murderer.

Prime Minister Nehru addressed the nation: 'Friends and comrades, the light has gone out of our lives and there is darkness everywhere.'

Gandhi was a saint, and the whole world was shocked at such a wicked act, but it did allow Nehru, Gandhi's political heir, to clamp down on militant Hinduism and reinforce the rule of Congress. The purpose of the assassination was to kill a peacemaker and to ignite a civil war. That did not happen: the assassins failed to achieve what they wanted.

Indira Gandhi
31 October 1984

'If I die today, every drop of my blood will invigorate the nation.'

Indira Gandhi, the daughter of Pandit Jawaharlal Nehru, was his personal secretary during his premiership from 1947 to 1967. She became the President of the Congress Party in 1959, and after the death of Nehru's successor, Shastri, in 1966 she became India's first female prime minister. The old Congress hands supported her in the belief that they would be able to control her. They could not have been more deluded: she soon exerted her own personal control over the whole range of government policy, and also became a well-known international figure who enhanced the status of India. She was very authoritarian, and for two years from 1975 to 1977 she instituted a state of emergency that increased her powers

'If I die today, every drop of my blood will invigorate the nation.'

to limit certain basic liberties and to censor the press. She was defeated in the election of 1977 and the new Government tried to convict both her and her son Sanjay for corruption, but in the election of 1980 she won by a landslide.

Indira Gandhi was passionately determined to retain India as one nation. She did not give an inch to pressure from Pakistan over the divided states of Punjab

The Golden Temple after the siege

and Kashmir. In 1982 the religious Sikh leader Bhindranwale with two hundred armed followers took control of the Golden Temple at Amritsar in the Punjab, the Sikhs' most holy shrine, and demanded autonomy. By 1983 the Temple had become a fort, as many more militants armed with machine guns had flocked there. After long and fruitless negotiations in 1984 Mrs Gandhi ordered the Indian Army to enter the Temple and arrest the militants. In their attack the army used tanks and heavy artillery, but the Sikhs fought back vigorously and the siege lasted for seven days. It was officially reported that 5,000 Sikh militants had been killed, and only 83 Indian soldiers. These figures were disputed, and some claimed that 20,000 Sikhs and 5,000 soldiers had been killed. As a result of the bombing the Temple itself and its famous library had been badly damaged. The leader of the militants, Bhindranwale, was killed. The Indians call him a terrorist, the Sikhs a saint. Sikhs across India and the world were appalled at this sacrilegious attack, for although it had succeeded in stopping an independence movement it hit at the very heart of the Sikh religion.

After this attack it was amazing that Indira still retained as part of her personal guard a number of Sikhs. Her security chief recommended their removal, but she insisted that they should remain to show to the world her tolerance and her desire to promote reconciliation. She fully appreciated the danger, and the very day before her assassination she said at a political meeting: 'If I die today, every drop of my blood will invigorate the nation.'

Some four months after the siege, on 31 October 1984, as she was walking to a meeting in Delhi with Peter Ustinov, the film director, two of her Sikh guards shot her – Beant Singh three times; Satwant Singh discharged thirty rounds into her body. They did not attempt to escape, and dropped their weapons. Beant was killed and Satwant injured.

This assassination did nothing to promote Sikh independence: after Indira Gandhi's cremation millions of Sikhs were displaced and 3,000 killed in anti-Sikh riots in Delhi and North India. These killings were organised by leading Congressmen. It was claimed that the number of dead rose to 8,000, which does raise the question of whether it was suppressing riots or genocide. In a report some four years later the Indian Home Office Minister acknowledged that a fuller investigation had uncovered a larger conspiracy, and that a foreign agency had persuaded the Sikhs to murder the Prime Minister.

Thirty-four-years later, in 2018, Sajjan Kumar, aged seventy-three, a former Congress Party MP, was sentenced to life imprisonment for the part he had played in the mass murder of Sikhs following the assassination. Kumar had led a

Sikhs protesting with anti-Gandhi banners

mob into south-west Delhi, and one Sikh woman described what had happened to her family: 'They broke down the door and killed my husband, my son went out of the house where another mob beat him with rods and then burnt him alive with kerosene oil. On the next morning another mob came in and burnt three brothers alive.' Kumar had been acquitted of all charges, but was found guilty of criminal conspiracy. At the time of the assassination of his mother, Rajiv Gandhi, explaining the killing, had said: 'When a big tree falls the earth shakes.' Rajiv himself was to be assassinated in 1991.

Rajiv Gandhi
21 May 1991

Rajiv was Nehru's grandson, but he was not interested in politics. Following the death in an aircraft of his younger, more politically active, brother Sanjay, he was asked to take on the role of leader of his family with the potential to become prime minister. He reached that post in 1984 after the assassination of his mother,

Two Congress ministers break down as they identify Rajiv Gandhi's body

Indira. The most successful project of his premiership was his policy to improve telecommunications and to sow the seeds of the Indian software industry in Bangalore and Hyderabad. His premiership was overshadowed by the Bofors scandal, where money from a Finnish company that had won a large contract had been diverted to the Congress Party. In international matters there was one step he took that was to seal his fate: he sent an Indian Peacekeeping Force into Sri Lanka to help the Government contain and defeat the Tamil Tigers, who were seeking to create an independent Tamil state.

On 21 May 1991 Rajiv was campaigning near Madras and walking to the platform through a dense crowd of supporters. A bespectacled woman in her thirties bowed down to kiss his feet, and then detonated a bomb hidden under her sari. Rajiv was killed instantly. The woman's head was blown off with her features undamaged, but her identity has never been discovered. The police believed from the start that it was an attack planned by the Tamil Tigers, though that was denied. After a ninety-day manhunt they identified the chief planner to be Raja Arumainayagam, known as 'One-Eyed Jack', the intelligence chief of the Tamil Tigers. His gang was eventually cornered in Bangalore; after a gun battle six of the Tamils took cyanide capsules and Raja shot himself.

This assassination did the Tamils no good: it reinforced the reputation of their movement to be violent, and that steeled the Sri Lankan Government to continue the fight, which in 2009 they eventually won.

Benazir Bhutto
27 December 2007

Benazir Bhutto was a beautiful and talented member of an aristocratic political family who decided to devote her life to politics. She went to both Harvard and Oxford, where she became the President of the world-renowned debating society, the Oxford Union. Her father, Zulfikar Bhutto, founded the Socialist People's Party of Pakistan (PPP); he became President of Pakistan in 1970 and in 1973 Prime Minister, but he was ousted by a military coup in 1977. In 1979 he was executed by hanging. His trial had been rigged by General Zia, the head of the army. On his death his wife and Benazir took over control of the Party.

Benazir was repeatedly imprisoned by Zia, and exiled to Britain in 1984. She returned in 1986 and transformed the PPP from a Socialist to a Liberal party. In 1988 she was the first woman to become prime minister of a Muslim country. However her reforms were turned down by the President, and a new party was formed, the Islamic Democratic Alliance (IJI). Its fundamentalists objected to her Western secular politics, and also accused her and her husband, Asif Ali Zardari, of corruption. Ousted by the army in 1990, she lost the election that followed which was rigged against her. The new government was also accused of corruption. and was dismissed after three years. Benazir won the election held in 1993. She survived for three years, but was dismissed as a result of a major bribery scandal operated by her husband. After losing the 1997 election she took refuge in Dubai. The activities of her husband, who had earned the nickname 'Mr Ten Percent', did nothing to improve her reputation.

Taken on the day of her death

As a result of American support, General Musharraf allowed Benazir to return to Pakistan in 2007 to fight the 2008 election. On a platform to improve women's rights, to contain the power of the army, and to resist fundamentalist Muslim violence, her campaign was a powder keg and complete anathema to radical Islam. She returned from her exile on 18 October 2007. Shortly after leaving the airport, en route to a rally in Karachi, two explosions occurred. She was not injured, but the explosions, later found to be a suicide bomb attack, killed 139 people and injured at least 450. On 27 December 2007, after a meeting with the President of Afghanistan, she made a speech at a large PPP rally in Rawalpindi. As she was leaving in her bulletproof car she opened the sunroof and stood up to wave to the crowd. A man standing just six feet from the car fired three gunshots at her and then detonated a suicide vest packed with ballbearings. She died on the way to hospital.

The Government claimed the assassin was a young boy from South

Waziristan; al-Qaeda also claimed credit, but the man most likely to have planned the assassination was Baitullah Mehsud (pp. 203-204), the leader of the Taliban, who knew that Bhutto's pro-American and secularist agenda would weaken Taliban control of South Waziristan. Mehsud had his own training programme for suicide bombers, but later he was to be killed by an American drone: those who live by assassination die by it – just as Shakespeare had forecast.

Five men alleged to be Taliban fighters were arrested and put on trial; it lasted for nine years, and they were then acquitted. The same court ordered that the assets of Musharraf should be confiscated and that he should be charged with conspiracy to murder as he did not provide adequate protection, but he had already fled to London.

Motorbike assassinations

I am indebted to a journalist in Bangalore, Sudipto Mondal, for information about assassinations in India by motorbike riders in addition to that of the investigative journalist Gauri Lankesh (pp. 236-237). In August 2013 Narendra Dabholkar, an atheist and a Dalit (Untouchable) campaigner against religious superstition, was shot from a motorbike. In February 2015 a Communist leader and journalist, Govind Pansare, was killed in a small town near Mumbai. And in August 2015 M. M. Kalburgi, an eminent intellectual and critic of idol worship, was shot. The purpose of these assassinations was to stifle dissent. The message was clear: 'Attack the government, step out of line and you will be shot.'

SRI LANKA

Lalith Athulathmudali
23 April 1993

Lalith was at Jesus College when I was at Magdalen and we got to know each other through the Oxford Union. Slim and handsome, he was a gifted debater; he became President of the Union, the first Sri Lankan to achieve that, and his English was so good it allowed him to be witty. He studied Law and then taught at several universities, including Singapore and Edinburgh, before he went into politics and entered parliament in Sri Lanka in 1977.

Lalith held several ministerial posts under the prime ministership of Jayewardene, particularly as Minister for National Security from 1984 to 1988, responsible for the military campaign against the Tamil separatist movement in north and east Sri Lanka. In the other posts he held he introduced a number of reforms, and he had become one of the most powerful and prominent ministers.

On Jaye Wardene's resignation in 1988 Lalith stood for the post of prime minister against Ranasinghe Premadasa and was defeated. There was no love lost between the two, deriving from their difference in status: Lalith was a member of the Govigama caste, the highest in Sinhalese society, whereas Premadasa belonged to the Dhobi or Washermen's caste, which was virtually the lowest. Lalith was offered the minor posts of Agriculture and then Education, which enabled him to reform the universities, but he had no respect for the Prime Minister. Together with a number of MPs he resigned when a move to impeach Premadasa on charges of illegal land-dealing and abuse of power failed. He also resigned from the United National Party and in 1991 formed the new Democratic United National Front. He was charismatic, and used his oratory to build up a strong personal following across the country. He announced that he would stand for the presidency in 1994.

Premadasa withdrew Lalith's police protection and had his home invaded by tax inspectors, who found nothing. On 23 April 1993 Lalith ended a long

Lalith and his daughter

day of campaigning by addressing a rally of one thousand at 8pm. Suddenly the electricity was cut off and a man ran forward, shooting him three times. Next day the body of a Tamil youth was found who had died of cyanide poisoning – a hallmark for Tamil terrorists. The police investigation named that man as the killer, but Lalith's family never accepted that.

A commission appointed by the new President in 1997 found that the youth had been made a scapegoat by a killer gang that had been put together by several prominent politicians and police officers. Premadasa must have known of the plot, which indeed he may have instigated, for he wanted his most serious political opponent out of the way. Several of the politicians and police officers who had been indicted mysteriously died before their trial. We will really never know who was directly responsible, for a week later Premadasa himself was assassinated by a Tamil terrorist.

A Tamil minister killed by a Tamil

Laksham Kadirgamar
12 August 2005

Laksham Kadirgamar was studying for a postgraduate degree in Law at Balliol College when I got to know him through the Oxford Union, and we met many times. An exceptionally good speaker, he made many friends and admirers that led to him becoming President of the Union – the second Sri Lankan to achieve that post.

On returning to Sri Lanka he qualified as a lawyer and built up a significant practice in commercial law. He also served on several international bodies. He decided to stand as an MP for the People's Alliance (PA) and won. Almost immediately he was appointed Foreign Secretary, a post he held for seven years, and during that time he managed to get the LTTE, the Tamil Tiger group, banned internationally. Laksham was one of the most significant politicians in Sri Lanka, and he took a very hard line against the Tamil Tigers, though he himself was a Tamil. When his Party won the election in 2004 he was in the running to become prime minister, but another colleague was appointed and he became Foreign Secretary again.

A year later, on 12 August 2005, while getting out of the swimming pool at his home, he was shot. No one believed LTTE's denial, but Laksham had said only a month earlier, 'They can get me at any time.' The police arrested two Tamils: one was the gardener of Laksham's neighbour, who admitted that he had let two assassins in.

VII

THE ASSASSINATION OF INVESTIGATIVE JOURNALISTS

'Assassination is the extreme form of censorship.'

GEORGE BERNARD SHAW

Despots who acquire power through an election soon fall out of love with democracy as it requires an active and critical opposition, and their first assault on democracy is to attack the free press. Ecuadorian President Rafael Correa called the media 'a grave political enemy that has to be defeated', and Turkey's President Erdogan accused journalists of propagating 'terrorism'. Russia's Putin threatened Vladimir Gusinsky, the owner of the independent NTV Media Network, with charges of 'financial misappropriation' unless he sold it for a song to Gazprom (he did, and fled from Russia). Venezuela's Hugo Chavez called his press critics 'enemies' and 'traitors' and forced media networks not to cover politics in their news. In Peru, Alberto Fujimori appointed the head of his Secret Service, Montesinos, to pay bribes to the media networks to sack investigative journalists and only air the news that he had approved. In Poland a Treasury Minister has been given the power to appoint the public heads of TV and radio networks and to grant advertising only to favoured networks. In his first year of office President Trump called the American media 'the enemy of the American people' and journalists 'amongst the most dishonest human beings on earth' – so it is not just despotic regimes that attack investigative journalists: demagogues can exist in all regimes.

A charity in France, Reporters Without Borders, publishes each year a World Press Freedom Index. In 2017 it found that the population of the world overwhelmingly lived in countries where there was little or no press freedom. English-speaking countries – the UK, North America, South Africa, Australia and New Zealand – and most of the countries of Europe allow journalists to file stories without fear of being arrested, tortured or killed. The Index also recorded that the number of journalists and media workers who had been killed had risen from 29 in 2002 to 69 in 2017.

I have included some of the most recent incidents where investigative journalists have been assassinated by the agents of a state. These targeted killings occur in countries as vast as Russia, China, Iran and Saudi Arabia, and as small as Malta and Slovakia. Even so, the West will only hear a relatively few little leaks from China and Iran, and it is known that in Russia the KGB and GRU have planned and carried out hundreds of killings which they have been able to hide. A list of people in the news world murdered in Russia between 1993 and 2009 amounted to 365. They included cameramen, freelance journalists, proofreaders, editors, film-makers, TV presenters and radio reporters. Most were shot in the street or outside their homes, but some were beaten to death, or run down by a vehicle, or stabbed.

Publicity in the West ensures that perpetrators are unmasked. In Malta the investigative journalist Daphne Galizia was blown up in her car in 2017 when she was investigating corruption in the Prime Minister's office, including his wife. Her assassination completely discredited the Prime Minister, and there have been calls for the United Nations to set up an independent inquiry, for Malta was revealed as the soft underbelly of Mafia corruption in Europe. In Slovakia the journalist Ján Kuciak and his fiancée were shot when they were investigating parts of the Government working with Italian gangs in syphoning off European Union agricultural and energy subsidies, building 'Palermo in Slovakia'. Within a week the Prime Minister had to resign. The editor of aktuality.sk, the news outlet for which Kuciak worked, said: 'Our message is that if you kill a journalist more will come out. They can't kill all of us.'

The Russian assassination of Georgi Markov and Alexander Litvinenko in London and the attempted assassination of the Skripals in Salisbury led to the identification of the assassins – it was a triumph of CCTV – and the trails led directly to Putin, who held himself up to ridicule when he boasted on TV that the two Russian assassins were tourists eager to visit Salisbury. That was a lie direct to camera, since he knew both were officers of the GRU, one of whom, Chepiga, had been highly decorated by himself. It is very rare for a head of state to expose himself so publicly in bare-faced lying.

Jamal Khashoggi, a mild critic of the Saudi regime, entered the Saudi Embassy in Turkey, was murdered, dismembered, and his remains placed in a suitcase and burnt in an oven. Up to that moment Crown Prince Mohammed bin-Salman had established a reputation as a progressive reformer bringing Saudi Arabia into the modern world, but his ruthless plan to eliminate Khashoggi revealed an unscrupulous, cruel and barbaric murderer. The trial of the so-called 'rogue officials' shows that justice in Saudi Arabia is still medieval, for the names of the accused have not been revealed and the trial is being held in secret. The lesson is clear: the assassination of investigative journalists will not protect corrupt, decadent and despotic regimes, since all the world will learn that they are in fact corrupt, decadent and despotic.

Georgi Markov
7 September 1978

Georgi Markov, a Bulgarian journalist, novelist and playwright, defected in 1968 when his latest play was banned by the Bulgarian dictator, President Todor Zhivkov, and sought asylum in London. He worked for the BBC World Service, the US-funded Radio Free Europe and Germany's Deutsche Welle, establishing a reputation for acerbic comments about the political regime in Bulgaria. His wife said that his comments on the Communist elite in Bulgaria were 'vitriolic' and with his comments on their sex lives he was 'smearing mud on the people in the inner circles'.

The intrepid critic

One of his principal targets was President Zhivkov, the longest serving leader in the Soviet bloc, who could not stand any critical opposition. Years later, in 1991, the KGB Major General Oleg Kalugin admitted in an interview that he had responded to a request for help from Zhivkov: he sent two KGB operatives to Sofia to provide the Bulgarian Secret Service with soluble pellets containing the poison ricin, to be concealed in a sharp umbrella tip.

On 7 September 1978 Markov was waiting for a bus to take him over Waterloo Bridge to the headquarters of the BBC at Bush House in the Strand when he felt a sharp sting to the back of his right thigh. He turned around and saw a man in the bus queue picking up an umbrella from the ground, who said he was sorry and disappeared into a taxi going in the opposite direction. Later that evening Markov became feverish, started to vomit, and became slowly stiffer. Dr Bernard Riley, who treated him in hospital, recalled: 'When I came in he was sitting up on the trolley. The first thing he said was, "I was warned three months ago they were out to get me, and I have been poisoned by the KGB. I am going to die and there is nothing you can do about it . . . The umbrella man could have been an assassin.'" The doctors were unable to trace the poison, but even if they had there was no antidote, and four days later he died.

MI5 and microbiological experts found in Markov's skin tissue a platinum iridium pellet smaller than the head of a pin which contained the deadly poison ricin. The pellet was ingeniously designed, with the ricin in tiny holes, with a coating that would melt at 37°C – the temperature of the human body. Such a device was beyond the medical and technical skills of Bulgaria: it had been designed and made by the KGB.

The 1.52mm diameter pellet that killed Georgi Markov

It was not the first time for the KGB to use this method of assassination. A few weeks earlier, in August, another Bulgarian defector, Vladimir Kostov, working in France, had fallen seriously ill after he was mysteriously hit in his back on a Paris Metro escalator. He did not die. An x-ray revealed that he was carrying a small pellet in his back. This was sent to London, and confirmed as being the same as the one that had killed Markov. The British police did identify Kostov's would-be assassin as Francesco Gullino, a Bulgarian spy living in Denmark, who travelled a lot in Europe as an art dealer, but he got away scot free.

A memorial day demonstration

Anna Politkovskaya
7 October 2006

Anna Politkovskaya was an independent journalist who fearlessly wrote articles about corruption in Chechnya, and the way its leader and the FSB (the Russian Federal Security Service) ignored all human rights and suppressed any opposition through arbitrary imprisonment, torture and assassination. To frighten her she had once been arrested and subjected to a mock execution, and another attempt was made with poisoned tea while on a plane to Chechnya. They eventually decided to kill her in the lift of her apartment block in Moscow on 7 October, Putin's birthday – a very loyal present.

Eight years later five men, principally from Chechnya, were found guilty of her murder, but who paid them has never been revealed or discovered.

Alexander Litvinenko
21 November 2006

Alexander Litvinenko had been a Russian spy working for the FSB. In 1998 he and other FSB officers accused their supervisors of organising the assassination of Boris Berezovsky, a Russian tycoon living in Britain (p. 141). Litvinenko had once been responsible for his security, though later he had received instructions to kill him. Litvinenko was then arrested and charged with exceeding his authority; unexpectedly he was acquitted, but then arrested again. In 2000 he decided to flee from Russia with his family and claim refugee status in Britain, where later he was recruited by MI6 as an expert on Russian organised crime.

He wrote several books accusing the Russian security services of staging events in an important building that were crucial to Putin's pathway to power. He also accused Putin of ordering the murder of the troublesome journalist Anna Politkovskaya.

He agreed to meet two former colleagues, Andrei Lugovoi and Dmitri Kovtun, for tea at the Millennium Hotel in Grosvenor Square, London, on 1 November 2006. He received several calls from Lugovoi seeking confirmation that he was coming. Lugovoi knew that he would not drink alcohol, so he had arranged a tea party. He said: 'There is still some tea left here, if you want you can have some' – a clever, disarming, comment implying that the others had already been drinking from the teapot, which they had not. Litvinenko poured out some tea into a clean mug. Later that day he fell ill and was soon in hospital. He described what had happened: 'I swallowed several times, but it was green tea with no sugar and it was already cold. Maybe in total I swallowed three or four times.'

The hospital could not find the cause of his illness. At first they thought it was thallium poisoning. Then forensic experts found that the china teapot gave readings of 100,000 becquerels of polonium per cm^2. In Kovtun's bathroom a lump of debris stuck in the wastepipe measured 390,000 becquerels. It was only a

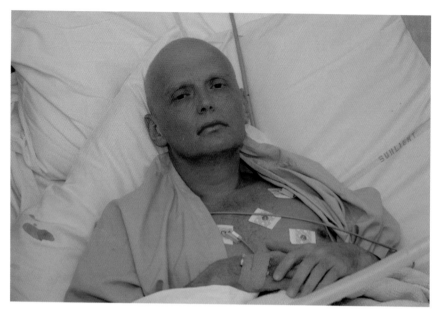

Litvinenko a few days before his death

The assassin – Andrei Lugovoi

few days before Litvinenko's death on 23 November that polonium was identified as the poison.

Litvinenko's widow campaigned vigorously to discover the culprits. An inquiry by the Home Office, opened in 2014, confirmed the guilt of Lugovoi and asked that he be extradited from Russia to be charged with murder – a useless request, as Russia does not allow any of its citizens to be extradited. The coroner's report, published in January 2016, concluded that Litvinenko had been murdered by an FSB operation that had probably been personally approved by Putin.

The assassination of Litvinenko, who had defected from Moscow to London, had the most significant consequence of any of the assassinations of investigative journalists because he did not die quickly but lived for a further twenty-two days, during which time he was able from his hospital bed to identify his murderers and to describe the way he was killed.

On their return to Russia both of the murderers were hospitalised for radiation treatment and claimed that MI6 was responsible. Three months after the assassination Lugovoi was placed on a candidates' list for the Russian Duma, which would give him political immunity. Interviewed by *El Pais* he said, 'If someone has caused the Russian State serious damage they should be exterminated.'

This was a state-sponsored murder where the perpetrators used such an unusual and unknown poison that they believed they could get away with it. The use of polonium would have been sanctioned by the very highest authority in Russia. The London Coroner was in no doubt that President Putin would have approved its use. For a head of state to be personally concerned about what an ex-spy could further reveal, after being in England for over five years, is paranoiac. Let Litvinenko have the last word, as he lay dying: 'You may be successful in silencing one man, but the howl of protest across the world, Mr Putin, will reverberate in your ears for the rest of your life.'

Marie Colvin
22 February 2012

Marie Colvin, a fifty-six-year-old American journalist for the *Sunday Times*, had covered conflicts in over fifteen war zones and was recognised as 'the greatest war correspondent of her generation'. Whenever there was a major crisis or war she just 'had to be there', always at the most dangerous point. She crossed into Syria on a motorcycle in 2012 and went immediately to the city of Homs which was under siege, surrounded by President Assad's troops supported by Iranian and Russian forces subjecting it to bombing every day. Colvin had acquired a sense of danger, and so with the British photographer Paul Conroy, who had tried to dissuade her, she went to Baba Amr, a suburb that was taking the heaviest shelling. She saw a tiny one-year-old baby die, and she wanted that story to get out on CNN so the White House would see it. 'It is so hard to witness what is going on here and I only have words. I will do one more week here and then leave. Every day is a horror.' On 22 February she filed what was to be her last report:

> The Syrians are not allowing civilians to leave. Anyone who gets into the street is hit by a shell. If they are not hit by a shell they are shot by snipers. There are snipers all around on the high buildings. I think the sickening thing is the completely merciless nature: they are hitting the civilian buildings absolutely mercilessly without caring and the scale of it is just shocking.

Assad's army had identified the exact location of her make-do media centre by tracking her phone satellite signals, as Colvin wanted to broadcast live to the BBC and CNN. This tragic fact was confirmed by a former Soviet intelligence officer who had defected. Conroy had learnt that the Syrian Government had ordered 'the killing of any Western journalists found in Homs'. The most instantly recognised was Marie, as she wore a piratical black eye-patch to cover a wound she had received in Sri Lanka. Artillery units on the edge of Homs then targeted

"The greatest war correspondent of her generation"

her, with a form of shelling known as 'bracketing': an observer reports on how close the shells are to the target, so they can adjust the range of the guns. The first bomb fell to the left, the second and third to the right; Conroy realised that the next would be right on target, so they tried to get out. That next bomb hit the front of the house just as Marie was running through it. As Paul crawled out of the building with a damaged leg, he saw Marie's head covered by rubble: she had been killed. A Syrian intelligence officer said: 'Marie Colvin was a dog and now she's dead. Let the Americans help her now.' She was sufficiently important for President Assad to add his comments: 'Marie Colvin had entered the country illegally and had worked with terrorists and was responsible for everything that befell her.'

All this information became known to the world when in 2018 her younger sister launched a court action in America to accuse the Syrian Government of Marie's assassination. Her lawyers had tracked down witnesses, experts and regime defectors to piece together how the Syrians had discovered her exact location. In 2019 the court found that a targeted attack, personally approved by Assad's more ruthless brother, Maher, had killed Marie. Judge Jackson imposed punitive damages of $300 million and awarded her sister $25 million for her personal loss. He said: 'Marie dedicated her life to fighting for justice on behalf of the victims of war – this case is an extension of her legacy.' Lawyers will now try to track down Assad's assets across the world, which are believed to be more than $1 billion. It also opens up the possibility of a criminal investigation by the Department of Justice under the War Crimes Acts, leading to indictments of members of the regime. Marie Colvin's assassination was definitely a poisoned chalice for the whole rotten regime. She is likely to have the last word: whenever the history of Assad's war upon his own people is written about, the picture of the woman with the black eye-patch will always be there, capturing with her own death the death of a city.

Colvin was quite fearless, driven by a duty to report the suffering and horrors of families destroyed by war, ethnic cleansing and vicious despots. The intensity of her life took its toll emotionally and physically, but she just would not give up. In one of the several award ceremonies which honoured her, she had said: 'Our mission is to speak the truth to power. We send home that first rough page of history. We do make a difference in exposing the horrors of war and especially the atrocities that befall civilians.'

Gauri Lankesh
5 September 2017

Gauri Lankesh, a popular journalist and editor of the tabloid *Gauri Lankesh Patrike*, a weekly newspaper published in Bangalore, was killed outside her home on 5 September 2017 by an assassin on a motorbike who fired seven shots, three of which entered her heart and lungs. She was an outspoken critic of Prime Minister Modi's Hindu nationalist Government, calling the rise of Hindu nationalism 'fascism'. She had started her career working for the *Times of India* and for the following thirty years she established a reputation for being outspoken and fearless.

She had organised several meetings and marches of the various groups opposing Modi – indigenous tribes, Dalits from the Untouchable castes, Leftists,

Supporters at a rally in Mumbai on the day after Gauri Lankesh was killed.

Christians and Muslims. She had a real flair for creating enemies. She was a member of the Lingayat community in Karnataka, which is separate from and opposed to Brahmanical Hinduism, and they threatened the Hindu nationalist BJP in the forthcoming state elections in Karnataka. Her murder showed India descending into violence.

Daphne Caruana Galizia
16 October 2017

On the afternoon of 16 October 2017 the leading investigative journalist in Malta, Daphne Caruana Galizia, who had just filed a hard-hitting blog about what Keith Schembri, the Chief of Staff to the Prime Minister Joseph Muscat, had been saying in a libel case, got into her rented Peugeot car to drive to the town of Mosta. A few hundred yards down the road there was a loud explosion: a bomb, which turned out to be using military grade Semtex, ripped open her car, throwing it off the road and scattering her body across a field.

She was Malta's most popular journalist, targeting alleged corrupt politicians and business people for money-laundering, having Mafia links, and an online gaming industry in a country that had 259 online betting firms. On some days her blogs had over 400,000 readers in a country of 420,000 people. Her lawyers said they were defending her in at least forty libel cases. Daphne had survived previous assassination attempts when her front door was set alight by car tyres and petrol.

Using material from the Panama Papers, the source of documents leaked from the Mossach Fonseca law firm, she discovered that officials in the Prime Minister's office and the Premier's wife had received money through companies they owned in Panama by granting a Maltese banking licence to the Azerbaijan royal family. Daphne also claimed that Prime Minister Muscat had put up for

sale Maltese passports for 650,000 euros: these could be snapped up by any Russian oligarch as that was the way to get to Paris, London and Berlin. She had also unearthed disturbing figures about the appointment of pro-Labour judges and investigators after Labour's victory in the election of 2013. The Government said that this only affected a third of the appointments, but she claimed it was double that.

Her targets were not just Labour Party ministers or MPs. She accused Adrian Delia, the leader of the opposition Nationalist Party, of having offshore accounts connected to prostitution in London, and also money

The fearless reporter exposing corruption

laundering. He responded by issuing five libel cases against her. She also accused a leading hotelier of corruptly acquiring land from the public sector for a new hotel.

She clearly had no friends in high places in Malta, for she revealed that the island was Europe's criminal underbelly. One of her blogs in 2016 said: 'Malta's public life is afflicted with dangerous unstable men with no principles or scruples.' One of her sons, who is also a journalist, commented: 'We are people against the state and organised crime which have become indistinguishable ... we are a Mafia state.'

After her death the Government offered a reward of $1.2 million for information leading to an arrest, and on 3 December 2017 the police announced the arrest of ten Maltese nationals. In December three men were charged with her murder. It has been revealed that one of them, Alfred Degiorgio, was seen both before and after the murder with the Maltese Economy Minister, Chris Cardona.

Daphne's last blog on the day she was assassinated was: 'There are crooks everywhere you look now. The situation is desperate.'

In August 2018 her family launched a campaign for an international inquiry into her death.

In June 2019 the Council of Europe representing forty-seven countries called for an independent inquiry into Galizia's death. They denounced 'a climate of impunity' over suspected corruption, and accused Prime Minister Muscat of offering 'personal protection' to officials over the alleged secret Panamanian bank accounts which were being investigated by the young journalist. The Strasbourg resolution also deplored the failure to bring the suspected murderers to trial: it raises 'serious questions about the rule of law in Malta'.

In November 2019 a leading tycoon, Yorgen Fenech, the richest man in Malta, was arrested as he was about to leave the island on his yacht. He was later charged with complicity in the murder of Daphne Galizia. Fenech asked for a presidential pardon by offering to cooperate with the investigation to reveal the influence of Keith Schembri, the Prime Minister's Chief-of-Staff, who had just resigned his post. The Tourism Minister Konrad Mizzi had also resigned as it was revealed that Daphne had uncovered that he and Schembri owned a company based in Panama which was set to receive US$2 million for undisclosed services from a Dubai company, 17 Black Limited, owned by Mr Fenech. The European Parliament sent an emergency team to investigate the rule-of-law in Malta and large street demonstrations demanded that Prime Minister Joseph Muscat must resign. He did so on 1 December, but said he would remain in post until 18 January 2020, which led to even greater demands for him to go at once. The assassination of Daphne Galizia was a poisoned chalice for both the Government and the reputation of Malta.

Ján Kuciak and Martina – "They can't kill all of us"

Mr Fico announces the reward, but it did not save him

Ján Kuciak
21 February 2018

On 24 February 2018 Peter Bàrdy, the Editor in Chief of Actuality, a team of Slovakian investigative journalists, was told that one of his employees had been killed. A twenty-seven-year-old reporter, Ján Kuciak, and his fiancée Martina Kušnírovà had been found murdered at their home in Vel'ká Mača, just forty miles east of the capital, Bratislava. When Bàrdy told his team of twenty-seven reporters – now alas only twenty-six – they decided as a tribute to edit and publish Kuciak's last unfinished investigation. Within forty-eight hours it was published, with Bàrdy saying: 'Our message is that if you kill a journalist more information will come out. They can't kill all of us.'

Kuciak had been investigating criminal gangs from Italy operating in the poorer eastern parts of Slovakia, tying up with local politicians, exploiting weak state institutions, syphoning off misappropriated European agricultural and energy subsidies and engaging in VAT scams. The Italian Mafia had infiltrated the politics of Slovakia.

Robert Fico, Prime Minister for ten of the last twelve years, had appointed Mária Trošková, a former topless model, as one of his assistants. Kuciak managed to find out that she had been a business partner of an Italian, Antonino Vadala, who had close ties to a notorious Italian crime group, the 'Ndrangheta. Mária had also worked with an MP, Viliam Jasaň. Vadala and some others were arrested. Fico's defence of Mária and Jasaň could not last, and they both had to stand down.

Fico offered a reward for further information about the journalist's death, but tens of thousands took to the streets in Bratislava and other towns calling for the resignation of the Coalition Government. A week later Mr Fico resigned his premiership, but he did stay on, saying: 'I want to be an active political party leader.' Most commentators assumed that he will be a backseat driver. One Slovak Facebook user said: 'The names on the doors have been changed, but the people in the background will remain the same.' Kuciak's former colleagues pledged to continue the investigation. As one said, 'The Mafia is doing business in this country and they have connections with the highest offices of state. They are building Palermo in Slovakia.'

In 2019 a Slovakian millionaire businessman, Marian Kočner, was charged with the murder of Kuciak and his fiancée. Kočner had previously threatened Kuciak, but the police had not followed this up as Kočner 'had influential friends in politics, the police and the prosecutors. They protected him.'

In March, in the first round of the presidential election, an anti-corruption lawyer, Zuzana Caputova, who had entered politics only one year earlier, ran a campaign tapping into the vein of horror at the murder of Kuciak and won 40.6 per cent of the votes cast, beating Robert Fico's presidential candidate. In the run-off a fortnight later she won 58.4 per cent of the vote. An amazing and unique result for a forty-five-year-old lawyer who had held no political post. It showed that the assassination of Kuciak and his fiancée was a poisoned chalice for the previous president and the corrupt circle around him.

Maksim Borodin
16 April 2018

Maksim Borodin, a thirty-two-year-old journalist who worked for the Russian newspaper *Novy Den* (New Day), fell to his death from his fifth-floor flat in Ekaterinburg. It seemed it was suicide. But the Editor of *Novy Den*, Polina Rumyantseva, said that Borodin was about to move to their Moscow office and that he planned to marry in the autumn: 'He had big life plans. I can't say he was depressed.' A friend, Polina Andreeva, said, 'I know for sure he was not planning to leave life behind, but to enjoy a bright future.'

The door to his flat was found to be locked from the inside; there was no suicide note; and there were no alcohol or drugs in his blood. Vyacheslav Bashkov, a friend of the journalist, said that Borodin had called him early on the morning of 11 April, saying that there was 'someone with a weapon on his balcony and people in camouflage and masks on the staircase landing'.

Borodin had recently filed a piece about Russian mercenaries in Syria killed

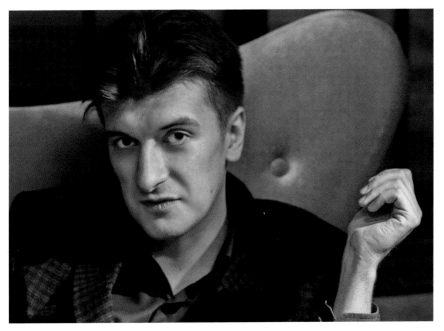

Maksim Borodin - thrown to his death

by American airstrikes. The official line from Moscow is that there are no Russian soldiers in Syria. Technically that is correct, as Yevgeny Prigozhin, a billionaire friend of Putin, had been asked to set up an agency to employ Russian mercenaries, and it was some of these who were killed by the airstrike. Mike Pompeo, the Head of the CIA, confirmed that about two hundred had been killed. The friends of the Liberal politician Boris Nemtsov thought that the interest he was showing about Russians killed in Ukraine, despite official denials of their presence, was the reason he was assassinated.

Assassination by being thrown out of a window or pushed over a balcony had been used before. In 2007 Ivan Safronov, a journalist from *Komersant* newspaper, fell to his death from a fifth-floor flat in Moscow, and his friends were convinced that he had been murdered. A team of assassins would sometimes threaten a victim by simply leaving a window open, indicating what might be their fate.

Jamal Khashoggi
2 October 2018

The distinguished fifty-nine-year-old Saudi journalist Jamal Khashoggi went to the Saudi Consulate in Istanbul on Tuesday 2 October 2018 to collect papers concerning divorce from his Saudi wife. He was accompanied by his fiancée, Hake Cengiz, who waited outside for him. Since then he has not been seen. It was revealed that a fifteen-man squad had arrived in Istanbul from Saudi Arabia that morning and had returned later the same day. The rumour quickly circulated that they had killed Khashoggi and taken back his body, possibly in parts. The Saudi Ambassador said nothing had happened and took journalists around the Consulate on Saturday – five days after it had been cleaned up. President Erdogan said the Saudis must produce Khashoggi, and CCTV footage was examined.

Khashoggi was a leading journalist, living in self-imposed exile in America and writing for the *Washington Post* about the internal workings of the Saudi inner circle, which was well known to him but impenetrable to the Western press. He had edited a Saudi paper and run a TV station in Saudi Arabia, but his

Last seen going into the Consulate in Istanbul

latest articles were highly critical of the regime and the new heir to the King, Prince Mohammed bin-Salman, who was being portrayed to the West as a great reformer. Khashoggi protested about the ruthless suppression of any dissenting views, and berated the Crown Prince for waging a bloody war in Yemen which he was starving into submission.

A man of this standing cannot simply disappear, and no one believes that he left the Consulate freely, as his fiancée would have seen him or heard from him. He was due to speak at a conference in Washington with other critics the following week. It is ironic that this disappearance of an investigative journalist, which caught the attention of the world, happened in Turkey, where the freedom of the press is curtailed and some journalists have been jailed.

Just three days before he disappeared, Khashoggi chatted to a BBC reporter: 'I do not think I will be able to go home. When I heard of the arrest of a friend who did nothing, it makes me feel like I shouldn't go. The people being arrested aren't even dissidents, they just have an independent mind.'

The Turkish Government let it be known that they had an aural and visual record of Khashoggi being tortured and then dismembered. They sent a copy to America, but it was not generally released, as it would show that the Turkish Government had bugging devices in the Consulate. Two weeks later the Saudi Government admitted that Khashoggi had been murdered in the Consulate, allegedly after a fist fight.

CCTV images were then published showing someone looking like Khashoggi and wearing his clothes leaving the Consulate and going to a café. A closer inspection showed he was wearing a false beard, and trainers, not Khashoggi's shoes – another amateurish bungle, a triumph for CCTV.

In October 2018 the Saudis changed their story yet again: Khashoggi had been killed by a rogue group acting on their own, eleven of whom had been arrested, and the Government was seeking the death penalty for five. In November the CIA, without telling President Trump, leaked that they had intercepted a telephone call from the Prince's younger brother, Prince Khalid, the Saudi Ambassador to Washington, to Khashoggi assuring him that he would

Peter Brookes, *The Times*, **18 November 2018**

be safe in going to the Consulate in Turkey to collect his divorce papers. Prince Khalid of course denied making the call, but it exists, and his brother clearly put him up to it. Trump said that he had been briefed about the recording of Khashoggi's murder, but he did not want to listen to it because it was clearly a 'suffering' tape. But anyway so what. Saudi Arabia was 'a truly spectacular ally'.

In December 2018 the CIA concluded with 'medium to high confidence' that Prince Mohammed 'personally targeted' Khashoggi and 'probably ordered his death'. The CIA had records of eleven messages – though not their contents – sent by Prince Mohammed bin-Salman to his close adviser Saud al-Qahtani, the man supposedly in charge of the Khashoggi operation in the hours before and after the killing. The CIA also had records of al-Qahtani overseeing a programme of abducting and torturing dissidents, including foreigners, and had explicitly sought approval from the Prince for previous 'sensitive missions'.

I understand from Lord Ramsbotham, a former Chief Inspector of Prisons and a former army general, that he had spoken to someone who had seen the video of the killing of Khashoggi, his dismemberment, and the dissolution of his body in acid.

A close colleague of Mohammed bin-Salman, Major General Ahmed al-Assiri, had been made the Deputy Head of the kingdom's spy agency – the General Intelligence Directorate – in 2017. He had attended meetings with businessmen who had proposed setting up a private company to assassinate overseas opponents, principally in Iran. In October al-Assiri was dismissed and named as the rogue leader who planned the murder of Khashoggi. You couldn't get closer to the Crown Prince than that. US intelligence agencies reported in 2019 that they had unearthed a call made a year before the assassination in which the Crown Prince had threatened to use a bullet on Khashoggi.

In March 2019 Al-Jazeera, the Qatari news organisation, revealed that in the previous October the Saudi Consul General in Istanbul had had built in his garden a tandoori oven which was exceptionally large and deep and able to burn at temperatures over 1,000°C – hot enough to melt metal. It claimed that Khashoggi's remains had been stashed in bags and driven in diplomatic vehicles to the garden oven. They also revealed that traces of Khashoggi's blood had been found in the Consul General's office after some fresh paint had been removed.

The Consul General's extra-large tandoori oven

Kateryna Handzyuk
31 July 2018

Kateryna Handzyuk graduated from the National Economic University in Kiev in 2003, and became a young politician in her home town of Kherson. She was an adviser to the Mayor, and after local elections in 2015 she became Manager of Affairs in the Council. She was an active civil rights and anti-corruption campaigner, and exposed corruption in the Regional Department of the Ministry of Internal Affairs of the Ukraine. She also publicised the involvement of the police in several cases of corruption in Kherson which meant that investigations were never completed.

As she left her home on 31 July a litre of sulphuric acid was thrown over her head and shoulders, damaging her eyes and causing severe burns to a third of her body. After three months in hospital she died. The President of the Ukraine, Petro Poroshenko, demanded that her attacker be brought to justice, but little progress was made. From her hospital bed Kateryna had claimed that the authorities and police were so intertwined with criminal gangs that they would not investigate this murderous assault. Other people protesting at illegal building contracts

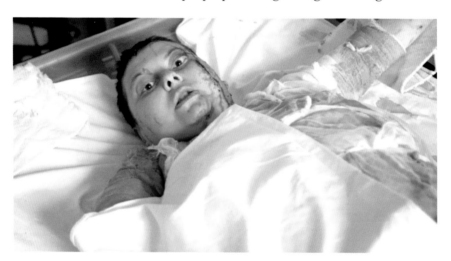

Burnt to death for exposing corruption

had been subjected to acid attacks, of which fifty-five since 2017 have remained unsolved. It would seem that corruption at all levels is endemic in the Ukraine.

Yuri Lutsenko, Ukraine's Chief Prosecutor, and the police have been attacked in parliament for not properly investigating this attack. He responded by accusing parliament of failing to sanction the arrest of MPs suspected of corruption. Kateryna Handzyuk's case was caught up in the battle for power in the impending elections.

Viktoria Marinova
6 October 2018

A new method of assassination of an investigative journalist occurred in Ruse in north-eastern Bulgaria in 2018. Viktoria Marinova, a thirty-year-old journalist, had just started as the host of TVN, a popular regional television station. She had

interviewed two journalists investigating the embezzlement of European Union funds on a TV show, Detector. Dimitar Stoyanov of the Bivol website and Attila Biro of the Romanian Rise Project investigative site alleged that a ring of consultancy firms were channelling EU investment funds to Bulgarian companies for kick-backs. Viktoria Marinova had said: 'The number of forbidden topics is growing all the time. Investigative journalists are being systematically removed.'

Viktoria Marinova

Viktoria Marinova's body was found near the Danube, where she had been jogging, on 6 October 2018. She had been raped, suffocated, and her face so broken that it was scarcely recognisable. Viktoria had told some friends that she had been stopped on the previous day when jogging by three men and an argument had ensued. The owner of the Bivol site said that his team had been threatened, and 'Viktoria's death, the brutal manner in which she was killed is an execution. It was meant to serve as an example, something like a warning.' The Bulgarian Interior Minister said there was no evidence to show a connection between Ms Marinova's work and her death. That denial is not surprising, because Bulgaria is the most corrupt country in the EU, and human rights organisations claim that there is collusion between politicians and the media. The Bulgarian Government announced within a few days that the culprit, who was a gipsy, had been discovered in Germany and they were seeking his extradition. We will have to wait and see. How did a gipsy know about Viktoria and where she was jogging, and how could he have suddenly got to Germany? How did the police manage to find him so quickly? In *The Independent* of 10 October 2018 the man is named as Severin Krasimirov. Bulgarian officials said he was known to police. He was detained in Stade, near Hamburg, where his mother is said to live. Viktoria Marinova's mobile phone, keys, glasses, and some of her clothes were missing, prosecutors say. Some of her personal belongings were allegedly found in his flat. Perhaps they were planted to attribute guilt?

Jagendra Singh
1 June 2019

'My father was one such rare person who exposed the truth.'

Jagendra Singh, a freelance journalist, had been investigating 'land-grabs' and the alleged illegal extraction of sand from the Garra River in Uttar Pradesh, India. Many states had prohibited the extraction of sand, as it resulted in erosion, floods and environmental damage. However the rewards were very great, and it attracted criminal activities. Since May 2019 Jagendra Singh had also been investigating the rape of a young worker who had learnt from a local court that her accusation against Rammurti Singh Verma, an Uttar Pradesh minister, was not going to be pursued. On 22 May Singh wrote a post saying that he was being harassed by police and politicians and that he feared he might be killed by Verma.

Jagendra Singh – burnt by the police

On 1 June a gang, including some police officers and criminals allegedly acting upon the instructions of Verma, entered Jagendra's home, poured petrol over him, and set him alight. He was taken to a hospital and lived until 8 June, so he was able to speak about his murderous assassins.

The Police Superintendent decided that the journalist had committed suicide. Following the public accusations by Jagendra, however, five officers were suspended. The investigation will continue – it is hoped by police from Delhi. The Chief Minister of Uttar Pradesh gave 3 million rupees (£34,000) to Jagendra's family, hoping they would accept the police verdict, but Jagendra's daughter would not touch the money, as her father was fighting for justice. She said: 'My father was one such rare person who exposed the truth.' Thirteen Indian journalists investigating damage to the environment have been killed in recent years.

EPILOGUE

Poisoned chalices

I have looked at well over a hundred assassinations of well-known personalities and have found that overwhelmingly assassinations were poisoned chalices. The murder of the victim did not precipitate a political change, and more often provoked public revulsion: the assassin's cause was damaged, not enhanced. Only a weak regime or government can accept the wilful murder of their leader or their people. The consequence is often more repressive measures and a commitment to deny assassins any victory – best summed up by Margaret Thatcher: 'Terrorist assassins must never, never, never be allowed to triumph. They must not prevail.'

The ambitions of assassins were often thwarted. By stabbing Jean Marat, a leading Jacobin, in July 1793, Charlotte Corday hoped to stem the flow of his opponents to the guillotine, but when Robespierre got control of the Committee of Public Safety a few weeks later he launched the Great Terror. The assassination of Abraham Lincoln in 1865 did not change the political future of America in any way: his magnificent successes in abolishing slavery and uniting the country were irreversible. It was a tragedy that such a great leader was killed, but it did not lead to a reversal of his historic achievements.

The Irish Nationalists who stabbed the Irish Secretary Lord Cavendish in Phoenix Park in 1882 hoped to force the British Government to reduce coercive measures and welcome the growing campaign for Home Rule advocated by Gladstone. But this brutal killing led to more coercive measures, and no progress was made to resolve the Irish problem for forty years. The revolutionary group that assassinated Tsar Alexander II in 1881 killed the most liberal leader

Russia had ever had: he abolished serfdom and was even preparing to share his sovereignty with an elected assembly – but his successor abandoned all of that. If a form of constitutional monarchy had emerged, the Bolshevik Revolution might never have happened?

The two Czech nationalists who murdered Reinhard Heydrich, the Nazi Protector of Bohemia and Moravia, hoped that his death would end the persecution and murder of many Czechs. However, Heydrich was Hitler's favourite – 'That man has a heart of iron' – and the Nazi reprisals were horrific.

When James Earl Ray shot Martin Luther King in 1968, he hoped that the death of its charismatic leader would fatally check the civil rights movement, but with King a martyr the movement became unstoppable. President Putin's targeted killings of investigative journalists and exiled dissidents were all so clumsily done, when they were meant to be secretive and clandestine operations, that they got worldwide coverage, revealing how despotic and undemocratic Russia had become. The assassination of the Saudi Arabian journalist Jamal Khashoggi revealed to the world that the heir apparent, Prince Mohammed bin-Salman, was not an enlightened reformer but a cruel and ruthless despot.

For all of these and many other assassinations, it was poisoned chalices all round.

World changers

All assassins believe that by killing their victim the world will be a better place, but they have a tendency to overrate the importance and power of their victim. I recall Tolstoy's comment in *War and Peace*: 'Great men are merely labels which are given to events.' As all assassinations are violent and unexpected they quickly attract the attention of the world, but there is a danger of overrating their importance as an event that can have significant consequences. Virtually all the assassinations I considered had little or no effect.

One assassination that did undoubtedly change the history of the world was that of Archduke Franz Ferdinand in Sarajevo in June 1914. If Gavrilo Princip's bullet had passed just one inch away from his neck Europe would not have been plunged into the First World War, which broke out a month later. A war might have started later when France, Great Britain and Russia could not contain Germany's growing militarism, but it would not have been started by an Austrian Army attacking Serbia. It was never the intention of Princip to precipitate a major conflict in Europe: he just wanted Bosnia to escape from the Austro-Hungarian Empire and become part of Serbia. This assassination had unintended consequences that overwhelmed the world.

There are some failed assassinations which, had they been successful, would have had a significant effect on the subsequent history of the world. On Christmas eve in 1800 Napoleon, First Consul, was due to visit the Opera House in Paris to hear Haydn's Creation. To get there his carriage had to travel through a narrow street, rue Saint-Nicaise. There two royalist terrorists had placed obstructions to delay the carriage, and a horse and cart carrying a 200lb bomb. One of Napoleon's outriders was able to clear a passage and Napoleon's carriage passed through quickly. The assassin had lit the fuse of the bomb too late to kill Napoleon, but it killed eight others.

In 1939 Hitler left a meeting in the beer cellar in Munich some thirteen minutes earlier than expected. If he had stayed, he would have been killed by a bomb planted directly behind where he had been speaking. He had no heir. Whether Goering, Himmler or the generals took over, one cannot predict what might have happened. None of them had Hitler's demonic mission to fight and conquer the whole of Europe or his demented passion to kill all Jews. History would have been different.

I have been asked whether there has ever been a virtuous assassination. I think it is possible, but it does not appear to have happened. However if any of the four murderous leaders of the twentieth century, Hitler, Stalin, Pol Pot and Mao Tse Tung, who were collectively guilty of the deaths of many millions, had been assassinated, the history of the world would have been different and better, because their power rested on their personal absolute authority. They were all subject to assassination attempts, but each took great care of his safety by ensuring that any potential opponents were killed.

Margaret Thatcher – a very different leader – had a lucky escape at the Conservative Party Conference in Brighton in 1984, when a bomb exploded on the hotel floor above her room. If she had been killed the next leader of the Tories would have been either Geoffrey Howe or Michael Heseltine, both devoted supporters of the Common Market and the European Union. There were no other contenders: Willie Whitelaw was in the Lords, Norman Tebbit was severely injured in the blast, Nigel Lawson had only been Chancellor for a year and his great career lay ahead of him, and Cecil Parkinson was no longer a contender after his affair with his secretary. The Eurosceptic Tory MPs were a very small handful barely known to the public. Labour might have become the Eurosceptic party, as they had fought the 1983 election on exiting Europe. It is tantalising to think that the Tories would have become the major Euro-fanatics and in that case there would have been no referendum, no Brexit.

Addendum 2020

As this book was going to the printers the most successful military commander in the Middle East, Qasem Soleimani, who led the Iranian forces in Syria and Iraq, was assassinated by an American drone attack on his motorcade as he left Baghdad Airport in the early morning of 3 January 2020. Soleimani had risen to be the head of the Revolutionary Guard in Iran, had become an icon, and was spoken of as a possible president. Soleimani had sponsored and helped Hezbollah in the Lebanon to attack Israel, had given essential support to the Shiite rebels in Yemen, had been a principal force in destroying ISIS, and had given military help to President Assad of Syria for his attacks on rebel held towns. He was ruthless and responsible for the deaths of many thousands of people, including hundreds of American civilians and soldiers.

President Trump, emboldened by the successful elimination of the former leader of ISIS, Abu Bakr al-Baghdadi, approved the assassination of Soleimani whom he accused of killing many Americans, Tweeting, "I wanted to stop a war. Not to start a war." Al-Baghdadi was no longer a significant leader, but Soleimani was the active leader and in total command of all the Shiite forces in the Middle East. He was America's principal enemy and by far the most significant figure to be killed by a drone. Previous American Presidents had considered assassinating Soleimani and in 2007 David Miliband, the British Foreign Secretary, had blocked an SAS assassination plan.

It is very difficult to discern what is America's strategy in the Middle East — some troops have been withdrawn, but now others are being sent there. I do not think this assassination will lead to a war as Iran would be defeated and bankrupted. The consequences are that there will be revenge attacks by Iran and its allies, but Trump has already said the USA has identified 52 potential targets in Iran if Americans are killed.

By the time this book is published in April 2020, it will be clear whether this assassination was a glancing blow or a poisoned chalice.

Alamut, the secret fortress of the Assassins

APPENDIX 1

A Note on the Word 'Assassin'

The Oxford English Dictionary's first definition of 'assassin' is: 'A hashish-eater. Certain Muslim fanatics in the time of the Crusades, who were sent forth by their sheikh, the "Old Man of the Mountains," to murder the Christian leaders.'

The 'Old Man of the Mountains' was Hasan-i-Sabbah, leader of the Persian Ismaili, who in 1094 refused to accept the leadership of the Sunni Caliph in Cairo. This created a major split in the Muslim religion, and the two sides became arch enemies. Hasan, a convert to Islam, became a very learned scholar, preacher and missionary, and founded a branch of Shia Islam, Nizari Ismaili.

By converting supporters in a remote mountain valley in northern Iran he was able to take ownership of an impregnable castle at Alamut, which became the seminary for his followers. He recruited many young men and trained them to obey implicitly the command of their religious leaders: to kill the leaders of other religions. This became a sacred duty, for which they were given golden daggers. They were not an army but a secret society of fanatical guerrillas, murdering anyone who would not go over to the Nizari Ismaili sect, and particularly caliphs and viziers. Hasan's followers worked through several countries in the Middle East, including Persia, Syria, Turkey and Egypt, and Christian crusaders came across them. This terrorist religious movement flourished for nearly two hundred years until the Mongols and the Mamluk Sultan Baibars in 1275 occupied Alamut. The Assassins then became a minor heretical group.

It is said that the word is derived from the Arabic word hashish, for an intoxicating powder made from leaves of the Indian hemp, whose users became known as 'hashashins'. Marco Polo came across assassins in Persia: he noted that many of the young were given a potion that lulled them to believe that what they were doing would lead to paradise. Very few written records exist of Hasan's movement, but it seems that a rate of pay came to be established for each assassination. Dante in the Inferno mentions 'the treacherous assassin', and a contemporary of his explained this reference as 'an assassin is someone who kills others for money'. That might have been the custom in the Middle East, but it has not been the motive for virtually any significant assassination in the rest of the world.

APPENDIX 2

Roman Emperors Assassinated

Causes of death of Roman Emperors
From 14 AD to 395 AD

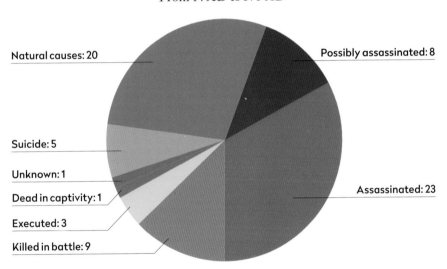

Natural causes: 20

Possibly assassinated: 8

Suicide: 5

Unknown: 1

Dead in captivity: 1

Assassinated: 23

Executed: 3

Killed in battle: 9

Of 71 Roman emperors 31 were assassinated, 13 by the Praetorian Guard. Assassination had become the way of disposing of an emperor who had become unpopular or who had failed to produce enough booty for his followers. Imperial Rome failed to find a way of transferring leadership without violence. The regime was inherently unstable: in one year, AD 69, there were four emperors: Galba, Otho, Aulus Vitellius and Vespasian.

PICTURE CREDITS

INDEX

Published in 2020 by
Unicorn, an imprint of Unicorn Publishing Group LLP
5 Newburgh Street
London
W1F 7RG

www.unicornpublishing.org

Text © Kenneth Baker
Images © see pages 262 – 263

ISBN 978-1-912690-75-6

10 9 8 7 6 5 4 3 2 1

Printed in Slovenia for Latitude Press Ltd